Thembalethu John Kumatana

Footsteps of Grace

In her footsteps, I find my way

A mother is her first son's true love - a love that is unwavering, unrelenting, and unconditional. A mother's love is the purest form of true love, and it's a gift that her first son will cherish forever."

I'd love to hear from you. Share your thoughts and feedback on my book by emailing

footstepsbookseries@gmail.com
facebook page:footsteps Book Series
Instagram:footstepsbooks
LinkIn:Footsteps Book Series

Copyright

Copyright 2025
Thembalethu John Kumatana

The right of Thembalethu John Kumatana
to be identified as the author of Footsteps of Grace
has asserted this work through the
Copyright, Designs and Patents Act 1988.

All Rights Reserved

No reproduction, copy or transmission of this publication
may be made without written permission.
No paragraph of this publication may be reproduced,
copied or transmitted save with the written permission of the
author or by the provisions
of the Copyright Act 1956 (as amended).

Any person who commits any unauthorised act about
this publication may be liable to criminal
prosecution and civil claims for damages.

First Published in 2025

Proof Reading and Editing by Busy Bee Editing
(www.busybeeediting.co.za)

About the Author

Thembalethu Johan Kumatana was born in Maclear on the 16th of September 1982 to his father, Bonisile Kumatana, and his mother, Nombulelo Kumatana. He is married to Nolusindiso Portia Kumatana. They are blessed with two beautiful, intelligent girls, Luphiwe Angela Kumatana and Alulutho Alison Kumatana. He attended public school in Maclean between 1989 - 1991 and Joelshoek Farm School between 1992 - 1993. He then moved to Elliot, where he attended Lundi Primary School between 1994 and 1997 and Masikhuthale Secondary School between 1998 and 2002.

After Matriculating in 2002, he moved to Cape Town to further his education. He attended Boland College Campus in Paarl as a part-time Human Resources student, doing evening classes and going from work to class from 2007 to 2010. He worked at different workplaces, but Fairview Wine Estate in Paarl was the most noticeable. He worked for Fairview from 2007-2016. He then started a Human Resources outsourcing company in 2016 with his business partner Estienne Venter and now finds himself the Director of a Human Resources company with his business partner Estienne Venter. Follow his series of 'Footsteps' books as he takes the reader on a mindful trip down memory lane and shares parts of his past that are genuinely made to inspire. In 2022, he enrolled at the Blackford Institute for Counsellors, studying for the counselling profession. His motivation to become a counsellor came from a deep-seated desire to help others navigate life's challenges, overcome obstacles, and achieve personal growth and healing.

Counsellors are driven by a passion for supporting individuals in their journey towards self-discovery, empowerment, and mental well-being. Thembalethu is motivated by the opportunity to positively impact people's lives by providing a safe space for clients to explore their thoughts and emotions, gain clarity, and develop coping strategies. The fulfilment from witnessing clients' progress, resilience, and transformation fuels counsellors' dedication to their profession, inspiring them to continue supporting and empowering others on their path to healing and self-improvement. Welcome to the introduction of ***Footsteps of Grace***. As we delve into the narrative, we are invited to reexamine our lives, reflect on our choices, and consider the fundamental aspects of our existence. Through their experiences, we find inspiration, guidance, and a renewed sense of purpose.

Table of Contents

Copyright 1
About the Author 2
Peface 7
What Is a Role Model? 9
My Mother, my Role Model, my Footsteps of Grace 12
My Mother's Selflessness 33
My Mother Taught Me to Value My Family 36
Love 38
My Mother Taught Me to Lead by Example 40
Patience in Life 43
My Mother Taught Me About Anger 46
Dealing with Challenges and Humbleness 49
 Room for Disappointment in My Life 51
Authenticity 53
Importance of Forgiveness 55
My Mother Taught Me to Be Open to Criticism ... 60
Importance of Clear Communication 62
Generosity and Kindness 65
Trust My Inner Voice 69
Hard Work and Commitment 72
My Mother's Concern Over My Upbringing 74
Value of Respect 77

My Mother Taught Me the Value of Responsibility, Trust and Accountability 80

Value of Commitment 83

Honesty and Humility 86

My Family Traditions 91

My Mother and God 94

My Mother Taught Me How to Pray 98

A Child Can Make a Big Mistake by Not Listening to Their Mother 101

Inheriting the Promises of God .**Error! Bookmark not defined.**

I Came Across the Book of Timothy 111

Footsteps of Grace 114

A Letter to My Mother 117

Preface

The book, 'Footsteps of Grace: A Journey of Mother and Son,' is a testament to the transformative power of the profound and enduring relationship between a mother and her son. It delves into the enriching experiences, challenges, and growth this relationship entails, inspiring you with the potential for growth in your own life. The narrative takes you on a heartfelt expedition through the cobblestone pathways of memory, revealing the depth and complexity of this unique bond. From the first tender embrace in a mother's arms to the proud moments of seeing her son flourish into a remarkable individual, this story encapsulates the universal truths of love, sacrifice, and unwavering support.

Through powerful narratives and thought-provoking reflections, *Footsteps of Grace* explores the joys and struggles that shape the mother-son dynamic, encouraging you to see the potential for growth in your relationships. It unravels the intricacies of a journey filled with laughter, tears, milestones, and life lessons, inspiring you to embrace the transformative power of your own experiences. This journey transcends the ordinary and creates an unbreakable bond that withstands the test of time. It is a tribute to the countless unsung heroes who have poured their hearts and souls into raising sons and nurturing them to become kind, compassionate, and confident individuals.

It celebrates the unspoken love between a mother and her son, forging an unbreakable connection that echoes throughout a lifetime. Join us on this emotional expedition as we delve deep into the unique relationship between motherhood and sonhood and discover the transformative potential within your relationships. This celebration of love and connection will leave you feeling warm and appreciative of the relationships in your own life.

What Is a Role Model?

A role model serves as a source of inspiration and influence on others. Role models are individuals who possess qualities that we admire and aspire to emulate in our own lives. Whether it be a celebrity, a parent, a teacher, or a friend, everyone has someone they look up to as a role model. In this book, we will explore the significance of having a role model and discuss the qualities that make someone a good role model. To begin with, having a role model is essential as it gives us a sense of direction and purpose in our lives. It guides how we should live and can inspire us to set and achieve our goals. A good role model can motivate us to work harder, be more disciplined, and strive for excellence in whatever we do. For example, a young athlete may look up to a professional sports player as their role model and be inspired to train harder and become their best.

Furthermore, role models help us to develop our values and beliefs. By observing how our role models conduct themselves and handle various situations, we learn what qualities are important to us and how we want to live our lives. For instance, children may have a parent as their role model and learn from them the importance of honesty, integrity, and hard work. This, in turn, helps them become better individuals and positively contribute to society. In addition, role models can provide us with a source of comfort and support during challenging times. When we face obstacles or setbacks, knowing that someone we admire has faced similar challenges and overcame them can give us the strength and courage to persevere. A role model can be a source of encouragement and motivation, helping us to stay focused on our goals and not give up when things get tough.

Now, let us discuss the qualities that make someone a good role model. Firstly, a good role model is someone who has achieved success through hard work and determination. Someone who has set high goals for themselves and worked tirelessly to achieve them. Their success should be in both their professional and personal lives, demonstrating a balance between work, family, and relationships. Secondly, a good role model should possess honesty, integrity, and compassion. They should do the right thing, even when difficult, and treat others respectfully and kindly. Role models should be people who stand up for their beliefs and are not afraid to speak out against injustice or wrongdoing. Furthermore, good role models should be humble and willing to admit mistakes. They should be open to feedback and criticism, constantly striving to improve themselves and learn from their experiences. Role models should be willing to share their knowledge and wisdom with others, acting as mentors and guides to those who look up to them. Role models are essential as they provide guidance, inspiration, and support. Whether it be a celebrity, a parent, a teacher, or a friend, everyone can benefit from having someone to look up to and aspire to emulate. A good role model is someone who has achieved success through hard work and determination, possesses qualities such as honesty and integrity, and is willing to share their knowledge and experiences with others. By emulating the qualities of our role models, we can become better individuals and make positive contributions to society.

My Mother, my Role Model, my Footsteps of Grace

Growing up in Maclear, my mother was the third youngest of eight children in a single-parent household. Life was tough for her family, with limited access to resources and opportunities. As the third born, my mother faced many challenges, including a lack of educational opportunities and having to work on farms to support the family. Being raised by a single mother in a rural area meant that my mother and her siblings had to learn to fend for themselves from a young age. With an absent father, their mother worked tirelessly to provide for her children. The family often struggled to make ends meet, with little money for necessities.

As the youngest, my mother usually felt the pressure of being the family's baby and felt the responsibility to help her older siblings in any way she could. Life in Maclear was not easy for my mother and her family. They lived in a small, cramped farmhouse with limited amenities. The siblings often had to share beds and rely on each other for emotional support. With no father figure present, my grandmother had to work long hours to make ends meet. This meant that the children often had to fend for themselves and take on responsibilities beyond the need to access educational opportunities. With limited financial resources, my mother and her siblings could only afford schooling up to a certain point. My mother had to drop out of school at a young age to help support the family. Despite her limited education, my mother was determined to make something of herself and work hard to provide a better future for her children.

Working on farms in Maclear was a common way for mothers like my mother and her siblings to earn money. They often helped at the farmers' houses, doing odd jobs in exchange for food and a small stipend. My mother missed out on valuable educational opportunities, as she had to prioritise work over school. However, the hard work instilled in her a strong work ethic and a determination to succeed. Despite her challenges, my mother never gave up on her dreams. She worked hard to provide for her family and create a better life for herself and her children. Through perseverance and determination, my mother overcame obstacles and built a better future for herself and her family.

When I think of outstanding leaders, my thoughts automatically turn to the current and previous presidents I have observed. With perhaps one or two exceptions, I cannot say that they epitomise a prominent leader. After consulting numerous definitions, I realised that they tended to describe a leader similarly, as someone who guides others. Thus, leaders do not necessarily have to be presidents; they could be teachers or parents. This realisation struck me when I recognised that a prominent leader was always right before me, imparting great values—my mother. During the past forty years, she has taught me so much, and only now do I realise that the noble qualities I possess as a man are thanks to her. Leaders invest their hearts and souls into their people and purpose, focusing on both aspects. My mother is the strongest woman I know. No matter the situation, she has always held her head high. She taught me that I can get through whatever life throws my way. This lesson has been more beneficial in my adult life than in my childhood, as there were many things I had not fully understood until now. Leaders maintain perspective, investing themselves entirely while keeping their priorities in order. As a child, I never grasped the reasons behind my mother's actions or words, but as an adult, I recognised that everything she did had a valid reason. Throughout my childhood, she shaped me into the man I am today, and I can pass on the lessons she taught me to my children. Successful leaders keep everything in perspective, distinguishing between what is essential and urgent and dedicating their time to others. My mother aspired to be a nurse and was very proficient in mathematics. However, her dreams were unattainable due to her upbringing on a farm by a single mother, my grandmother. She shared stories of the farm owner's wife, who was fond of her and wanted her to pursue an education. Yet, this opportunity was lost when the couple divorced. My grandmother worked in the farmer's kitchen, leading to my mother helping on busy days, which caused her schoolwork to suffer. She also had to milk cows when her brothers were unavailable.

Due to traditional practices in the African culture, one morning, she saw three old men approaching her homestead, whom she described as very unattractive. These men had come to ask for her hand in marriage. Fortuitously, while making coffee, she overheard their conversation with the elders and learnt they had come for her. Her brother helped her escape on a bicycle early in the morning as these men planned to intercept her on her way from school. With her brother's assistance, she fled to Umtata, where her older sister was working, and she did not return until she met my father, leading to the birth of my siblings and me.

When I transitioned from grade 5 to grade 6 in 1994, my family moved to Elliot. Unfortunately, I was unable to secure a spot in any school there. At the time, my father worked in the mines. I clearly remember that on the 4th of April 1994, during the Easter Weekend, I visited my aunt in the locations. My father, also in the area, chose not to see me. On his way back to Johannesburg, where he worked, the Vaal Maseru bus he was on was involved in an accident between Elliot and Indwe. Miraculously, my father was one of the three survivors. He was airlifted to Cecilia Makiwane Hospital in East London, where he underwent treatment and observation for over six months. During this period, my mother had to support my siblings and me without having a job, relying on the generosity of family members despite us having no relatives in Elliot.

We lived in a one-room mud house, a testament to the resilience and leadership of my mother, who was truly 'my rock.' This African house, constructed from soil and maintained with cow dung for cleanliness, represents a traditional and sustainable architectural form prevalent across Africa for centuries. Built from locally sourced materials like clay, sand, and organic matter such as straw or grass, these houses are well-adapted to the local climate and environment. Interestingly, the application of cow dung is practical and deeply ingrained in cultural traditions. With my father hospitalised, my mother took charge of constructing an additional two-bedroom house. Her leadership ensured my father's absence was hardly felt, thanks to her strength and presence. Eventually, she found employment at a clothing store.

Upon my father's return from the hospital, she would hand over her entire salary to him, demonstrating deep respect and teamwork in managing our household finances. This respect and the actions of my parents significantly influenced my understanding of responsibility and partnership. My mother also played a vital role in our community, contributing to neighbours' needs during funerals with food parcels or labour. She imparted crucial life skills to us from a young age, teaching us to do laundry, iron, cook, and wash dishes, emphasising that in her house, tasks were assigned based on need, not gender. This philosophy made me feel particularly targeted, but I am grateful for these lessons. I proudly admit that my mother profoundly influenced my life and worldview. She has been a relentless fighter, a beacon of goodness, and a source of unconditional love and forgiveness. Her teachings on God's nature and the world's realities have shaped me into who I am today. Despite numerous challenges, my mother's unwavering support throughout my life highlights her incredible strength and independence. When I passed grade 5 and was advancing to grade 6 in 1994, my parents relocated to Elliot. Unfortunately, I did not secure a place in a school there. During this period, my father worked in the mines.

My mother spearheaded a project to build another two-bedroom house while my dad was hospitalised. She kept our family going, and we hardly noticed our father's absence due to her strength and presence. Construction involves gathering suitable earth materials like clay, sand, and organic matter like straw or grass, mixed with water to create a malleable mixture for shaping walls, floors, and other structural elements. Cow dung's use for cleanliness in these mud houses is practical and deeply ingrained in cultural traditions and beliefs. Eventually, my mother secured a job in a clothing shop.

When my father returned from the hospital, she would bring home her entire salary, handing it over to him for joint financial decisions. This demonstrated respect and influenced my values. Parents often teach more through actions than words. My mother played a significant role in our community, contributing to neighbours during funerals through food parcels or labour and teaching us life skills and survival tactics from a young age, including laundry, ironing, cooking, and dishwashing. She emphasised that in our household, tasks were assigned based on need rather than gender, and she often felt like I was her main target. Now, I am grateful for all of it. I proudly acknowledge that my mother profoundly influences my life and worldview. She was a fighter in every sense, maintaining her strength even during difficult times in her marriage and teaching us about the nature of God, the importance of standing up for what is right, and the power of forgiveness.

My mother's unwavering support has guided me through life's hurdles to become who I am today. My worldview, instilled by my mother, is that God is our creator and overseer, and we are here to serve Him and others. Humanity, though inherently good, is capable of evil due to the fall of man, necessitating vigilance against such evils and a willingness to forgive. We must remain steadfast in our faith that God will restore inherent goodness in humanity, a belief I hold dear. The term "mother" encompasses all the world's children, representing a divine, selfless presence in our lives.

A mother's lap is our first school, profoundly influencing our character and thoughts. The significance of a mother's role cannot be overstated, as a mother represents a blessing more significant than a thousand others. Life without a mother is unimaginable, underscoring the need to recognise and appreciate mothers' importance. Mothers stand by us through thick and thin, their love and care unmatched. This deep bond between a mother and her child underscores a mother's unique and invaluable role in our lives, making the world more prosperous for their presence.

A mother loves her children immensely. She often wears old clothes herself while ensuring that her children have new ones. Considering it a matter of pride, she might sleep in a damp spot to ensure her children can sleep comfortably. Being blessed with a mother is seen as a fortune. A mother eagerly awaits her children's return from school, ready to feed them and inquire about their day and whether they ate at school.

A mother's capacity to do anything for her children knows no bounds. Even if she is momentarily upset with a child, she cannot bear to remain silent for long. She fasts tirelessly for her children's happiness, enduring days without food or water, believing God manifests as a mother to offer us protection. A mother is deeply invested in her children's futures, unparalleled in her love and concern. She cherishes her children but is ready to correct them if they stray, embodying a unique blend of love and discipline.

Without a mother, the world feels barren. The term 'mother' is not just a name but is the foundation of our existence. Life without a mother is unimaginable. Our day does not truly begin until we hear our mother's voice. She comforts us through illness and shares in our joys while understanding our preferences and dislikes. Mothers guide their children towards the right path, encouraging them to pursue the right direction. As our first teacher, a mother imparts lessons on all aspects of life, helping us differentiate between right and wrong. Motherhood represents an unparalleled bond, a complex and deep connection that no other relationship can match.

A mother's love is instinctual and protective. She ensures her children's safety and well-being while providing guidance and support. She is a constant presence, instilling values, morals, and beliefs and shaping her children into responsible members of society. A mother's love is empathetic and compassionate. She resonates with her children's emotions, celebrating their joys as if they were hers and empathising with their pain.

This unconditional support provides a haven for her children, fostering resilience and reassuring them that they are never alone. Over and over, a mother's love proves its boundless nature. It transcends distance and time and is steadfast even when physical separation occurs. A mother's love remains a constant comfort and reassurance whether children are near or far. This unbreakable bond strengthens connections regardless of circumstances. A mother's love extends beyond her biological children, offering care and nurturing to those in need. It recognises no bounds, seeing promise and potential in every child. As children grow and mature, a mother's love evolves alongside them. It adapts to their changing needs, guiding them while allowing them to forge their paths. A mother's love is not possessive or controlling but empowering, encouraging her children to explore their passions and fulfil their dreams. In moments of success, a mother's pride shines brightly. In times of failure and despair, her love is a comforting embrace, reminding her children of their worth.

A mother's love is eternal, transcending the boundaries of life and death. Even after a mother passes away, her love lives on in the hearts and memories of her children, becoming a guiding light and a source of strength in times of need. A mother's love leaves an indelible mark, shaping her children for the better.

A mother's love for her children can never be fully captured or described in mere words. It is a multifaceted emotion that defies explanation, a force that shapes lives, builds character and creates bonds that endure. It embodies the selflessness, compassion, and unconditional affection within each of us. Mothers play a pivotal role in the lives of their families, often juggling multiple responsibilities and commitments. Despite their selfless efforts and unwavering dedication, mothers often face challenges that can undermine their well-being and contributions.

Respecting mothers is not merely a gesture of appreciation but an essential element for fostering healthy family dynamics and ensuring the overall well-being of all family members. Recognising mothers' unique understanding and profound insight into their families allows us to tap into a valuable resource of knowledge and wisdom. Their attentiveness often leads to practical solutions to problems. Disregarding mothers' opinions and perspectives can lead to frustration, stress, and emotional exhaustion, restricting the potential for creative problem-solving that benefits the entire family.

Acknowledging mothers' insights, involving them in decision-making, and considering their emotional and practical well-being is crucial. When a mother's opinions, concerns, or advice are consistently disregarded, she may feel undervalued, frustrated, and ignored, leading to resentment and impaired communication. If a mother's voice is not heard, open and effective communication within the family may suffer, resulting in misunderstandings, conflicts, and a breakdown in trust and harmony.

Mothers, often their children's primary caregivers and nurturers, provide invaluable life lessons, moral teachings, and guidance for making informed decisions. Ignoring their voice can burden them more, leading to increased stress and feelings of isolation. Mothers often possess a unique and deep understanding of their family dynamics and individual members. Families may miss out on innovative ideas and alternative solutions by not listening to them. Recognising that every family and situation is different, the consequences of not listening can vary, but overall, they can negatively impact the well-being and dynamics of the family unit. Mothers deserve respect and inclusion in decision-making processes, fostering a healthy environment that supports and nurtures every family member. The relationship between a mother and her firstborn male child is complex and holds significant importance in many cultures worldwide, including African societies.

This bond transcends the biological connection, involving emotional, psychological, and social dimensions that shape the lives of both mother and child. The firstborn male child is often seen as the carrier of the family lineage and legacy, a role that stems from the deeply rooted traditions and expectations within these communities. From pregnancy, a mother may develop a strong emotional attachment to her unborn child, dreaming and aspiring for his future. The birth of a firstborn male child is met with societal recognition and gatherings, reinforcing his importance. The mother feels a profound sense of pride and fulfilment, which reflects positively on her and her role within the family.

In children's early years, the mother's role in nurturing, caring for, and teaching them is crucial for their development. She becomes a child's first teacher, imparting cultural values, traditions, and knowledge passed through generations. This relationship evolves as the child grows, with the mother providing guidance, wisdom, and support, becoming a constant source of advice and encouragement as they navigate life's complexities.

While marked by unconditional love and protection, the relationship between a mother and her firstborn male child may also be characterised by a sense of pressure and high expectations. The firstborn male is often tasked with carrying the family's legacy, which can weigh heavily on his shoulders. Understanding this, a mother endeavours to balance nurturing her child's connection to their cultural heritage with supporting his dreams and aspirations.

The bond between a mother and her firstborn male child is profound, built on a foundation of sacrifice and unconditional love. This love becomes a source of strength for the child, providing a stable base for his life.

However, it is essential to recognise that the dynamics of this relationship can vary widely across different African countries, ethnic groups, and even within individual families. As societal norms evolve, the traditional expectations placed on firstborn males may shift, influencing the roles and the pressures associated with this position.

In fostering a relationship filled with guidance, love, and support, a mother lays the groundwork for her firstborn male child's future, preparing him to carry his family's legacy forward with pride. This relationship involves not only the preservation of cultural heritage but also the nurturing of the child's own goals and aspirations. Mothers play multifaceted roles in their children's lives, from being their first teacher to their constant protector. The love a mother has for her children is unparalleled, offering unconditional care, support, and selflessness even before birth. This pure, unwavering love makes a mother's bond with her children unique and irreplaceable. Mothers are indeed guardian angels, always there to love, support, and protect their offspring. This special place a child holds in their heart for their mother is the foundation of an enduring attachment, highlighting the profound impact a mother has on her child's life.

However, only some are fortunate enough to experience a mother's love throughout their lives. For those with their mother by their side, it is crucial to cherish, love, and respect her, recognising her invaluable role. A mother can shape her children's future, influencing their character, habits, and outlook. Children seek their mother's approval and care deeply about her thoughts and feelings towards them, underscoring the significant impact a mother has on shaping their self-esteem. Mothers, whether stay-at-home, working, or juggling both roles, make tireless efforts daily to serve as role models for their children.

To a child, a mother is akin to a deity, making it imperative to inspire and encourage her child positively. The sense of security a mother provides is unparalleled, often being the first person, a child turns to in times of fear or uncertainty. The presence of a mother offers comfort and reassurance, making her an essential figure in a child's life from the beginning.

A child's physical and emotional growth heavily relies on their bond with their parents. The absence of parents or their failure to spend adequate time with their children can significantly hamper emotional development and behaviour. Children may experience a range of negative emotions such as depression, anxiety, low self-esteem, feelings of worthlessness, and even anger. Furthermore, parental absence can lead to issues in forming social connections due to trust concerns, as children might need to develop adequate social skills or may become overly dependent on anyone who offers them attention, regardless of its nature.

Becoming a mother fundamentally transforms a woman's life, presenting various challenges and surprises from pregnancy to the first encounter with her child. This transformation involves adapting to the role of a mother. A mother's bond with her child is naturally strong, making her a pivotal figure in her growth and development and allowing her to fulfil various crucial roles in their life. A mother is her child's first best friend and a mentor who consistently encourages and supports her children in achieving their aspirations. An effective mentor teaches the difference between right and wrong, offers encouragement, and provides necessary accountability. Mothers often embody these qualities, making a mother's love the purest form of love and a child's greatest blessing from God. The child must acknowledge the mother's sacrifices and efforts, as she desires nothing more than her child's success. Being blessed with a mother in our lives, we owe it to honour and respect her, showing her the love and happiness she deserves for her selfless dedication.

"A mother is her son's first true love; a son is his mother's last true love." This saying highlights the profound bond between a mother and her son, illustrating that a mother's heart is a rich source of learning for her child. I am immensely grateful for everything my mother has done for me. Her example of a godly mother fills me with pride, and I am honoured to be her son. I want to share several lessons I learnt from my mother that have significantly impacted me. These insights shaped my character and can serve as valuable lessons for other parents to impart to their children.

My mother stressed the importance of having a relationship with God, telling me, "Son, without God, you are nothing. You may run fast, get good grades, and achieve many things. But He is everything you need. You are nothing without Him." Teaching children to cultivate a relationship with God is perhaps the most crucial lesson a mother can pass on. My mother also taught me the value of endurance. She advised my sister and me never to give up, no matter the circumstances. We faced numerous challenges growing up, but my mother's perseverance taught us to continue pressing forward, even through difficult times. A child's physical and emotional development heavily relies on their relationship with their parents. When parents are absent or fail to spend adequate time with their children, it can detrimentally affect their emotional growth and behaviour.

Children may experience depression, anxiety, low self-esteem, feelings of worthlessness, and even anger. Parental absence can also lead to difficulties in forming social connections due to trust issues, potentially resulting in children's inability to forge meaningful relationships or becoming overly dependent on any attention they receive, whether positive or negative.

Becoming a mother transforms a woman's life, introducing her to various challenges and surprises from pregnancy to the first encounter with her child. This transformation includes adapting to the role of a mother, which is inherently natural yet profoundly significant. A mother can significantly influence her child's development and play various crucial roles in their life. A mother is not just the first best friend of a child but also a mentor who consistently encourages and aids her children in achieving their ambitions. An exemplary mentor teaches the difference between right and wrong, provides motivation, and holds you accountable when necessary. Our mothers often embody these qualities. Motherly love is the purest form of love, making a child's mother the greatest blessing from God. A child must acknowledge a mother's sacrifices and efforts, as her primary desire is her child's success. We are fortunate to have mothers who deserve our respect and love for their selfless devotion.

The saying "A mother is her son's first true love; a son is his mother's last true love" reflects the deep bond between mothers and their children. A mother's heart is often said to be the child's classroom. I am thankful for everything my mom, has taught me. I learnt the importance of having a relationship with God, endurance through hard times without magnifying the sacrifice, faithfulness, the power of prayer, the need to minister to others even in our own need, the distinction between right and wrong, and the essence of God-king love.

My mother's teachings and faith have significantly shaped my life, guiding me through my mistakes and leading me back on the right path. Her strength and softness, constant support, and guidance are invaluable. A mother's presence is irreplaceable, offering unwavering support and guidance through life's journey. No words can fully capture the essence of a mother's role and profound impact on our lives.

My mother has made countless sacrifices for my happiness. The love and affection she gives me are boundless. I love her deeply, as I do my father. My mother has been the most significant influence on me throughout my life. Through her example, I have learnt how to navigate the complexities of life. She is the one person I trust implicitly. She has been the driving force behind my progress and development, working tirelessly without ever showing partiality within our family. She provides all of us with equal, undivided devotion and love. Her commitment to our family is unwavering, often setting aside her needs and desires for our sake. My mother has inspired my spiritual, emotional, and intellectual growth, making her my most significant source of inspiration.

Mothers embody love and dedication. They are marked by their forgiving nature and understanding when we err. They take decisive action to correct our mistakes, ensuring we understand our responsibilities. From dawn till dusk, a mother works relentlessly to realise our dreams, consoling us in need, sacrificing for our comfort, and illuminating our lives with happiness and love like the sun dispels darkness.

Motivation, a crucial state of mind for accomplishing tasks, is often inspired by people or events. It fosters physical and social development, enabling us to achieve goals even in adversity. We seek encouragement from various sources, including influential figures or those close to us who believe in our potential despite challenges.

Mothers are an endless source of inspiration and motivation, instilling in us a sense of responsibility, care for others, and unparalleled resilience. Everyone needs a source of creativity and inspiration to achieve their life goals and progress. While a teacher or a successful individual may inspire some, my mother is my greatest motivation. She has encouraged me to pursue my life's objectives tirelessly. My mother's approach to life is also admirable. Unlike many who seek recognition or social status, she works selflessly to see her children succeed. Her lack of self-interest in her endeavours positions her as a living embodiment of divine grace. My mother is my teacher, adviser, and best friend, playing crucial roles in my life. She instils confidence in me during challenging times. Everything I have become today is directly attributable to her presence in my life, as she has supported me through my successes and failures.

I cannot imagine my life without her, so I regard her as my closest companion. Despite the numerous roles a woman assumes throughout her life, the bond shared with her son is among the purest forms of relationships in the world. The connection between a mother and her child is beyond words. A mother not only gives birth and raises her child but also harbours an everlasting love for her children, prioritising their well-being above hers. A mother is prepared to confront the greatest adversities to protect her child and is willing to bear all burdens alone to shield her offspring from hardships. For these reasons, mothers are often seen as earthly manifestations of God, leading to the saying, "God cannot be everywhere, and therefore he created mothers."

Although my mother may not be the strongest physically, she faces every challenge in her life and that of her family with resilience. She is a constant source of inspiration, urging me never to surrender to adversity. Moreover, my mother is a significant source of motivation, encouraging me to enhance my skills, academic achievements, and talents. She inspires me to persist, never to concede defeat, and to work diligently until I succeed. Observing her navigate the myriad challenges she encounters reminds us of a woman's strength and capability to withstand any trial. In times of trouble, my mom is my beacon of hope.

Despite her reprimands and corrections, she is the sole person capable of resolving school or life-related issues. She guides and leads me through the most challenging times as my mentor and adviser. Above all, she remains by my side even in the darkest moments. She is an outstanding teacher, a strict yet fair parent, a faithful friend, and delightful company. Every mother, embodying God's essence, dedicates her life to her family and deserves immense respect and admiration. A mother embodies both innate and acquired qualities that define her role. The fundamental characteristic of a mother is her sense of responsibility, which accompanies motherhood. My mother exhibits unconditional love and affection regardless of the circumstances, exemplifying the selfless nature of maternal love.

My Mother's Selflessness

My mother has always been a selfless and compassionate person who is always willing to lend a helping hand to those in need. Her kindness and generosity know no bounds, and it is no surprise that she has dedicated much of her time and energy to assisting the less fortunate in our community. One instance that stands out is when my mother took it upon herself to help people in need without asking for anything in return. One of our neighbours lost his wife, and they were unemployed. She took some groceries from our home and donated them to the neighbours to ensure that they food for their visitors.

My mother's heart went out to this family, and she immediately acted. My mother is a woman like no other. She is the summary of selflessness and compassion, always putting the needs of others before her own. When she became a mother, her focus shifted entirely to her children, sacrificing her wants and desires to ensure we were always cared for. Her unwavering love and dedication to her family are unparalleled, and I am constantly surprised by her strength and resilience.

Growing up, my mother was always there for me, no matter what. Whether I needed help with my homework, a shoulder to cry on, or someone to talk to, she was always by my side, ready to lend a listening ear and offer words of wisdom. She taught me the value of hard work and perseverance, instilling a solid work ethic that has carried me through some of the most challenging times in my life. My mother always put our needs ahead of hers, often going without so we could have everything we needed.

I remember times when she would skip meals or wear clothes that were falling apart so my siblings and I could have food on the table and clothes on our backs. Her sacrifices did not go unnoticed, and I am forever grateful for everything she has done for our family.

As I grew older and started my own family, I truly understood the depth of my mother's love and selflessness. Watching her handle my children with the same level of care and devotion that she showed me as a child, I realised just how fortunate I am to have her in my life. She is the rock of our family, the glue that holds us all together in times of joy and sorrow. My mother is a pillar of strength, a beacon of light in times of darkness. When I feel lost or overwhelmed, she is always there to offer guidance and support, and her calming presence gives me the courage to face challenges. Her wisdom and grace have been a constant source of inspiration for me, and I strive every day to be the kind of parent she is to me.

No words can adequately express my love and gratitude for my mother. She is an incredible woman, a true embodiment of selflessness and compassion. Her love knows no bounds; her generosity is endless. I can only hope to be half the person she is, to possess even a fraction of her strength and resilience.

My mother is a remarkable woman who has always put the needs of others before her own. Her selfless acts of love and sacrifice have shaped me into the person I am today, and for that, I am eternally grateful. I am blessed to have such a fantastic role model, and I can only hope one day to show her the same level of love and devotion she has shown me. She is my rock, my inspiration, my everything.

My Mother Taught Me to Value My Family

Family is one of the most important aspects of my life, thanks to the valuable lessons my mother taught me from an early age. Growing up, my mother instilled in me the importance of cherishing and valuing the bonds we share with our family members. She taught me that family is not just about blood relations but the love and support we give and receive from those closest to us. Through her actions and words, my mother showed me the true meaning of family and why it is essential to prioritise and nurture these connections throughout our lives.

My mother has always been the foundation of our family. She is a constant source of love, strength, and guidance for me and my siblings. From a young age, she taught us the value of being there for each other, no matter our challenges. Whether we were going through tough times or celebrating our achievements, my mother was always there to support and remind us of the importance of sticking together as a family. One of the most important lessons my mother taught me is the value of communication and open dialogue within the family. She encouraged us to share our thoughts, feelings, and concerns, believing that honest and open communication is the key to building strong and healthy relationships.

My mother always ensured we had time to sit together as a family and discuss our day, dreams, and fears. Through these conversations, we learnt to listen, empathise with each other's struggles, and offer support and encouragement. My mother also taught me the importance of forgiveness and acceptance within the family. She believed that no one is perfect, and we all make mistakes sometimes. Rather than holding grudges or harbouring resentment, my mother taught us to forgive, to let go of the past, and to move forward with love and compassion. She showed us that we can build deeper connections and create a more supportive and nurturing family environment by accepting each other's flaws and shortcomings. As I grew older, I came to appreciate even more the lessons my mother had taught me about the importance of family. In a constantly changing and evolving world, our relationships with family members remain one of our few constants. My mother's teachings have helped me to stay grounded and connected to my roots, even as I navigate the challenges and uncertainties of adulthood.

My mother's teachings about family have shaped the person I am today. I am grateful for the love, support, and guidance she has always provided me and the lessons she has imparted about valuing and cherishing our family connections. As I look towards the future, I will continue to hold dear the values and teachings my mother instilled in me and pass on these lessons to future generations. Family is the bedrock of our lives, and we must nurture and prioritise these relationships to lead fulfilling and meaningful lives. Thanks to my mother's teachings, I have the tools and values necessary to do just that.

My Mother Taught Me to Love

Love is an essential element in our lives that shapes our relationships and interactions with others. It is a powerful force that can unite people, heal wounds, and create a sense of belonging and connection. Many people's first experience of love comes from their parents, especially their mother. Mothers played a crucial role in shaping me to understand love and relationships. The love we receive from our mothers often sets the foundation for how we love others. I have been fortunate enough to have a loving and caring mother who has been a guiding light in my life.

From a young age, she has showered me with love, affection, and support, teaching me the true meaning of unconditional love. Her love has been my rock, haven, and source of strength to carry me through life's difficulties. I have always admired my mother's grace, patience, and unwavering love for our family. Watching her navigate life's challenges with grace and love has inspired me, and I am grateful for the lessons she taught me about love and compassion.

As I grew older and began navigating my relationships, I realised that the love I received from my mother profoundly impacted how I approached love. My mother's love had set a high standard for me, and I found myself looking for those same qualities in a partner. I wanted someone kind, compassionate, understanding, and supportive like my mother. I wanted a partner who would love me unconditionally, just as my mother had loved me. I wanted a relationship built on trust, respect, and mutual admiration.

When I met my wife, I knew she was the one for me. She possessed all the qualities I had learnt to value from my mother, and I felt a deep connection with her from the beginning. As our relationship grew and flourished, I realised that my love for my wife was an extension of the love I had received from my mother. Loving my wife felt natural and effortless, and I knew it was because of the love and guidance I had received from my mother that I could love her so deeply. I understand that the love we receive from our parents, especially our mothers, plays a significant role in shaping our capacity to love others. Our parents are our first teachers of love, and the love we receive from them forms the foundation for how we navigate our relationships and interactions with others. If I had not received the love and affection from my mother that I did, I do not believe that I would have been able to love my wife in the same way.

My mother's love has been a guiding force in my life, and I am grateful for the lessons she has taught me about love, compassion, and grace. Her love has shaped me into the person I am today, and I know that I would not be able to love my wife as deeply and fully as I do without the love I received from my mother. Loving my mother has been my *Footsteps of Grace* and has opened the door for me to love my wife with all my heart. The love I received from my parents, especially my mother's, plays a crucial role in shaping our ability to love others. The love I received from my mother has been a source of strength, guidance, and inspiration in my life, and it has enabled me to love my wife with all my heart. I am thankful for the lessons my mother has taught me about love and compassion, and I know that her love will continue to guide me in my relationships and interactions with others.

Loving my mother has been my foundation, allowing me to love my wife with the same grace and devotion my mother has shown me. Love truly is a powerful force that shapes our lives and relationships, and I am grateful for the love I have received from my mother, which has enabled me to love my wife so deeply.

My Mother Taught Me to Be an Example to My Siblings

Growing up in a large household with three younger siblings, I quickly learnt the importance of setting a good example. My mother, a strong and wise woman, instilled in me the value of being a role model for my brothers and sisters. Through her guidance and teachings, I have understood how my actions and words impact those around me, especially my younger siblings. My mother always emphasised the responsibility of being the eldest of four children. She taught me that my siblings look up to me and often model their behaviour after mine. As their older brother, my duty was to lead by example and show them the right path to follow. That meant making good choices, treating others with kindness and respect, and always striving to do my best in everything I did.

One of the most important lessons my mother taught me was the power of positive influence. She believed that the way I carried myself and the values I upheld would directly impact my siblings. If I demonstrated honesty, integrity, and hard work, my siblings would be more likely to do the same. My mother made it clear that I had the potential to shape their beliefs, attitudes, and actions through my behaviour.

My mother's teachings were not just words; she also led by example. She constantly inspired me and my siblings, always displaying grace, strength, and compassion in everything she did. Whether it was caring for our family, excelling in her career, or helping others in need, my mother embodied the qualities she wanted us to emulate. She showed us that being a role model meant living out our values and beliefs daily, even when faced with challenges or adversity. As I grew older, I began to appreciate my mother's guidance's impact on me and my siblings. I realised that being a role model was about setting a good example and being a source of support, encouragement, and guidance for those who looked up to me.

My mother taught me that being a positive influence meant being there for my siblings when they needed me, listening to their concerns, and offering advice and guidance whenever possible. One of the most important ways I have been able to be a role model for my siblings is through my academic and personal achievements. My mother always stressed the importance of education and hard work and encouraged me to strive for excellence in everything I did. By excelling in school, pursuing my passions, and setting goals, I have shown my siblings the value of determination, perseverance, and self-discipline. In addition to my academic achievements, I have tried to lead by example through my actions and behaviour. I treat others with kindness and respect, to be honest and trustworthy, and to always stand up for what I believe in. I positively influence my siblings by demonstrating good communication skills, problem-solving abilities, and leadership qualities.

Being a role model for my siblings has been challenging. It has required patience, understanding, and a willingness to admit my faults and shortcomings. There have been times when I have made mistakes, fallen short of my expectations, or struggled to live up to the standards set by my mother. However, I have always strived to learn from my failures, grow from my experiences, and become stronger and more determined to be the best brother and role model I could.

Reflecting on my upbringing and my mother's lessons about being a role model for my siblings, I am grateful for her guidance and support. Through her words and actions, my mother showed me the importance of setting an excellent example of being a source of inspiration and advice for those who look up to me. I want to continue honouring her teachings and positively influencing my siblings, helping them become the best version of themselves and achieve their goals and dreams. My mother taught me the value of being a role model for my siblings, leading by example and showing them the right path to follow. Through her guidance and teachings, I have learnt the power of positive influence and the impact of my actions and words on those around me. I am grateful for the lessons my mother has taught me, and I will continue to strive to be the best brother and role model I can be for my siblings.

My Mother Taught Me About Patience in Life

Patience is a virtue that my mother has always emphasised to me from a young age. She would often repeat the phrase, "Good things come to those who wait," to remind me that I must be patient and not expect everything to come to me instantly. This lesson has stayed with me throughout my life and shaped my approach to challenges and setbacks. Growing up, I was a very impatient child. I often got frustrated when things did not go my way, or I had to wait for something I wanted. My mother always told me that patience is critical to success and that I must learn to wait for the right opportunity. Initially, I did not fully grasp the importance of patience, but as I grew older, I started to understand the wisdom behind my mother's words.

One of the biggest lessons my mother taught me about patience was that only some things will happen according to my timeline. Life has its way of unfolding, and I must learn to adapt and be patient during difficult times. Whether waiting for a promotion at work, dealing with personal relationships, or pursuing my goals, my mother always reminded me to be patient and trust the process.

In today's fast-paced world, it is easy to get caught up in the hustle and bustle of everyday life. We live in a society that values instant gratification, where we can have anything, we want at the touch of a button. However, my mother has taught me that true success and fulfilment come from patience and perseverance. Staying focused on long-term goals and not getting discouraged by short-term setbacks is essential. Patience also teaches us the art of acceptance and tolerance. Life is unpredictable, and we may encounter obstacles and challenges that test our patience. Instead of resisting or fighting against these challenges, my mother taught me to embrace them with grace and composure instead of resisting or fighting them.

By practising patience, I have learnt to be more understanding and empathetic towards others and to approach difficult situations calmly and collectedly. My mother's teachings on patience have profoundly impacted my personal and professional life. In my career, I have learnt to be patient when working towards my goals and not to rush the process. I have experienced setbacks and failures but have overcome these obstacles and grown stronger through patience and persistence. In my relationships, patience has helped me navigate difficult times and communicate effectively with others. By being patient and understanding, I have built more profound connections with those around me and learnt to appreciate patience's value in fostering strong relationships.

Overall, my mother's lessons on patience have shaped me into a more resilient and compassionate individual. I have learnt that patience is not just about waiting for things to happen but also about trusting in the journey and believing in oneself. By embracing patience in all aspects of my life, I have overcome challenges, achieved my goals, and cultivate a sense of inner peace and contentment.

Patience is a valuable virtue that my mother instilled in me from a young age. Through her guidance and wisdom, I have learnt to be patient in all aspects of my life and to trust in the process. Patience has taught me the power of resilience, acceptance, and grace and has helped me become a better person. I am grateful for my mother's teachings on patience, as they have been instrumental in shaping the person I am today.

My Mother Taught Me About Anger

Anger is a powerful and often uncontrollable emotion that can lead to detrimental consequences if not appropriately managed. I have learnt this lesson firsthand through the wise words and guidance of my mother, who has always warned me about the dangers of acting out of anger. Growing up, my mother always reminded me to think before I speak or act when angry. She would tell me that anger is a temporary emotion that can cloud our judgement and lead us to make regrettable decisions. I remember one specific incident when I was a teenager and had an intense argument with a friend. I was so consumed by anger that I said hurtful things that I later regretted. My mother sat me down afterwards and explained to me the importance of controlling my emotions and thinking before I reacted in moments of anger.

My mother's warning about acting out of anger has stuck with me throughout my life, and I have realised the truth behind her words. Anger is a natural response to feeling hurt, frustrated, or threatened, but it is essential to remember that how we respond to our anger can make all the difference. Acting impulsively out of anger can have lasting consequences that we may later come to regret. I have witnessed firsthand the destructive power of anger in my personal life and the world around me. I have seen relationships destroyed, friendships severed, and even physical harm done because of uncontrolled anger.

When anger consumes us, we lose sight of reason and empathy and ultimately become prisoners to our emotions. My mother's warnings about the results of anger have taught me to take a step back and assess situations before reacting in anger. She has shown me that we can channel our anger into more productive outlets, such as communication, problem-solving, or self-reflection.

By pausing and collecting our thoughts, we can prevent ourselves from making impulsive decisions that we may later regret. In my own life, I have found that practising mindfulness and self-awareness has been instrumental in helping me manage my anger. By recognising the signs of anger early on, I can take a step back, breathe, and think before I act. I have learnt to express my feelings calmly and constructively rather than lashing out in anger.

My mother's warnings about acting out anger taught me the importance of forgiveness and empathy. Holding onto anger and resentment only breeds negativity and bitterness, harming us more than anyone else. By letting go of grudges and practising forgiveness, we free ourselves from anger and open ourselves up to healing and growth. I have realised that anger is a natural and inevitable part of being human, but how we respond to our anger defines who we are.

My mother's warnings about the consequences of anger have shaped me into a more thoughtful, compassionate, and emotionally intelligent individual. I strive to approach every situation with a sense of calm and understanding and to handle conflicts with grace and wisdom. My mother's warnings about acting out of anger have provided a valuable lesson that has guided me through life's difficulties. I have learnt to recognise and manage my anger healthily and to approach conflicts with a sense of mindfulness and empathy. By heeding her advice, I have navigated challenging situations with grace and wisdom and cultivated stronger, more meaningful relationships. Anger may be powerful, but we can learn to harness its energy positively and constructively with practice and self-awareness.

Dealing with Challenges and Humbleness

My mother instilled in me the importance of facing challenges head-on and with a sense of humility. She often said, "Life is full of obstacles, but how you respond to them truly matters." These words of wisdom have stuck with me throughout my life and guided me in difficult times and adversity. Dealing with challenges can be daunting, especially when they seem impossible to overcome. It is easy to become overwhelmed and discouraged when faced with obstacles, but my mother's words have taught me to approach challenges with a positive mindset and a humble attitude. Instead of letting fear and doubt consume me, I have learnt to tackle challenges confidently and gracefully.

One of the most valuable lessons my mother taught me is the importance of humility in the face of challenges. She often said, "Pride comes before a fall," reminding me that arrogance and self-importance can hinder overcoming obstacles. Instead, she encouraged me to remain humble and open-minded, willing to learn from my mistakes and grow from them. Facing challenges with humbleness also means acknowledging that I may not have all the answers or solutions right away. It is okay to seek help and guidance from others, to admit when I am struggling, and to be open to new perspectives and ideas. Humility growth. I have realised that anger is a natural and inevitable part of being human, but how we respond to our anger defines who we are.

My mother's warnings about the consequences of anger have shaped me into a more thoughtful, compassionate, and emotionally intelligent individual. I strive to approach every situation with a sense of calm and understanding and to handle conflicts with grace and wisdom. My mother's warnings about acting out of anger have provided a valuable lesson that has guided me through life's difficulties. I have learnt to recognise and manage my anger healthily and to approach conflicts with a sense of mindfulness and empathy. By heeding her advice, I have navigated challenging situations with grace and wisdom and cultivated stronger, more meaningful relationships. Anger may be powerful, but we can learn to harness its energy positively and constructively with practice and self-awareness.

Dealing with Challenges and Humbleness

My mother instilled in me the importance of facing challenges head-on and with a sense of humility. She often said, "Life is full of obstacles, but how you respond to them truly matters." These words of wisdom have stuck with me throughout my life and guided me in difficult times and adversity. Dealing with challenges can be daunting, especially when they seem impossible to overcome. It is easy to become overwhelmed and discouraged when faced with obstacles, but my mother's words have taught me to approach challenges with a positive mindset and a humble attitude. Instead of letting fear and doubt consume me, I have learnt to tackle challenges confidently and gracefully.

One of the most valuable lessons my mother taught me is the importance of humility in the face of challenges. She often said, "Pride comes before a fall," reminding me that arrogance and self-importance can hinder overcoming obstacles. Instead, she encouraged me to remain humble and open-minded, willing to learn from my mistakes and grow from them. Facing challenges with humbleness also means acknowledging that I may not have all the answers or solutions right away. It is okay to seek help and guidance from others, to admit when I am struggling, and to be open to new perspectives and ideas. Humility enables me to approach challenges with openness and curiosity, and I am eager to learn and grow through adversity. My mother's teachings on dealing with challenges with humbleness have served me well in various aspects of my life. In my academic pursuits, professional career, and personal relationships, I have learnt to confront challenges gracefully and poised. By embracing humility, I have overcome obstacles with resilience and determination. In times of difficulty, I often reflect on my mother's words and the lessons she imparted to me. I remind myself that challenges are a natural part of life and that how I respond to them reflects my character and values.

By approaching challenges with humility, I can maintain a sense of perspective and remain grounded in adversity. Dealing with challenges head-on and humbleness is not always easy, but it is a valuable skill that can be cultivated over time. It requires a willingness to step outside one's comfort zone, embrace vulnerability and uncertainty, and trust in one's ability to navigate difficult times. By adopting a humble attitude towards challenges, I have learnt to let go of my ego and instead focus on growth and self-improvement. My mother's wise words have shaped my approach to life's challenges. I have overcome adversity with resilience and grace by embracing humility and facing obstacles head-on. I am grateful for the lessons my mother has taught me and strive to embody her teachings in all aspects of my life. As I navigate life's challenges, I will never forget to approach them with humility and a positive mindset.

My Mother Taught Me to Always Leave Room for Disappointment in My Life

My mother has always been my guiding light, who taught me valuable life lessons and shaped me into who I am today. One of the most important lessons she imparted to me was always leaving room for disappointment. This lesson has been ingrained in me since I was a child, and it has guided me through many challenging situations and helped me to navigate life's difficulties. Growing up, my mother always emphasised the importance of managing expectations and being prepared for the unexpected. She often told me, "Life is full of good and bad surprises. It is important to be realistic and not set yourself up for disappointment by expecting everything to go perfectly."

I did not fully grasp the significance of her words then, but as I grew older, I began to understand their wisdom. As I entered my teenage years, I faced my fair share of disappointments – failed exams, rejection from colleges, heartbreaks. I recalled my mother's words in these situations and reminded myself to accept the disappointment and move on. Rather than dwelling on the negative outcome, I focused on learning from my mistakes, picking myself up, and moving forward with renewed strength and determination.

My mother's guidance taught me to embrace disappointment as a catalyst for personal growth and resilience. Rather than viewing it as a roadblock, I saw it as an opportunity for self-reflection and introspection. Each disappointment became a valuable lesson, teaching me humility, patience, and the importance of perseverance in the face of adversity. As I embarked on my journey into adulthood, the lessons my mother instilled in me continued to shape my outlook on life. I learnt to approach challenges with an open mind, understanding that setbacks are inevitable in the human experience.

By leaving room for disappointment, I acquired a sense of resilience and adaptability that has served me well in my personal and professional endeavours. I have encountered numerous setbacks and failures in my career, from rejected job applications to unsuccessful projects. However, instead of viewing these disappointments as defeats, I have embraced them as opportunities for growth and self-improvement. I have learnt to approach each setback with a sense of optimism and determination, knowing that with perseverance and hard work, I can overcome any obstacle that comes my way. My mother's lesson of leaving room for disappointment has not only helped me navigate the challenges of life but has also enabled me to forge deeper connections with those around me.

By accepting the imperfections and uncertainties of life, I have learnt to appreciate the beauty of resilience and vulnerability and to empathise with others who may be facing struggles and disappointments. Reflecting on my mother's wisdom impacts my life. I am filled with gratitude and admiration for the woman who has been my rock and source of strength. Through her guidance, I have embraced the inevitability of disappointment and learnt to navigate life's uncertainties with grace and resilience. I am forever grateful for the invaluable lessons she imparted to me, and I carry them with me as I continue to grow and evolve on my journey through life.

My Mother Taught Me About Authenticity

My mother has always been my biggest role model and inspiration in life. From a young age, she instilled in me the importance of always being authentic. She taught me that being true to myself, and my values and beliefs is essential to living a fulfilling and genuine life. One of the most important lessons my mother taught me about authenticity is always being honest with myself and others. She emphasised the importance of being true to my thoughts and feelings, even when it may be difficult or uncomfortable. My mother taught me that honesty is the foundation of trust and integrity and is crucial in building strong and meaningful relationships with others.

My mother also taught me the importance of staying true to my values and beliefs, even when faced with challenges or obstacles. She encouraged me to stand up for my beliefs and never compromise my principles to fit in or please others. My mother taught me that staying authentic to myself and what I believe in is the key to living a purposeful and meaningful life. Another important lesson my mother taught me about authenticity is being true to my emotions and feelings. She encouraged me to express my emotions openly and honestly, without fear of judgement or rejection. My mother taught me that it is okay to feel vulnerable and emotional and that by embracing and accepting my emotions, I will be able to understand myself better and connect with others on a deeper level. My mother also taught me the importance of being true to my dreams and aspirations. She encouraged me to pursue my passions and goals confidently and determined, even when faced with doubts and uncertainties.

My mother taught me that I can live authentically and genuinely by staying true to my dreams and working hard to achieve them. One of the most valuable lessons my mother taught me about authenticity was the importance of accepting and loving myself for who I am. She taught me to embrace my strengths and weaknesses and to be proud of the unique qualities that make me who I am. My mother taught me that self-acceptance is the key to building self-confidence and living a life that is true to oneself.

In addition to teaching me the importance of always being authentic, my mother also led by example. She demonstrated authenticity in her actions and words, showing me how to live a life of honesty, integrity, and genuine self-expression. My mother's authenticity inspired me to strive for the same level of genuineness and to always stay true to who I am and what I believe in.

My mother has been a guiding light regarding the importance of authenticity. She taught me to be honest with myself and others, to stay true to my values and beliefs, and to embrace my emotions and dreams with confidence and determination. My mother showed me by example how to live a life that is genuine, meaningful, and true to myself. I am forever grateful for the lessons she taught me about authenticity, and I strive to embody these values in everything I do.

My Mother Taught Me the Importance of Forgiveness

Growing up, my mother taught me the belief that holding onto anger and resentment only hurt me overall. She would always remind me that forgiveness does not excuse the wrong that someone has done, but rather, it frees me from the burden of carrying around hatred and negativity. One incident that genuinely embodied my mother's teachings on forgiveness stands out in my memory. I was in high school at the time, and there was a classmate who had been bullying me and others and forcing me to take his money home, and then we would use our lunch to make peace with each other. When I confided in my mother about the situation, she listened attentively and calmly said, "Forgiveness is not for the other person but for yourself. Holding onto anger will only poison your heart and soul." Her words struck a chord with me, and I forgave my classmate. It was challenging and did not happen overnight, but I let go of my anger and resentment over time. I realised that holding onto those negative emotions only brought me down and hindered my happiness. My mother's example of forgiveness did not just apply to others but to herself. She openly shared with me her own experiences of forgiving those who had wronged her in the past. She told me how liberating it was to let go of grudges and move forward with a clean heart.

I witnessed firsthand how my mother's ability to forgive allowed her to live a more peaceful and fulfilling life. She never allowed bitterness or resentment to consume her, and she always chose to see the good in others, even those who had wronged her. As I grew older, I faced more challenges and conflicts that tested my forgiving ability.

My mother's teachings on forgiveness guided me through the process each time.

I learnt that forgiveness is a choice; it takes strength and courage to forgive those who have hurt us. I also understood that forgiveness does not mean forgetting or condoning the actions of others. It simply means letting go of the negative emotions that hold us back and prevent us from moving forward. My mother's constant reminder to forgive has profoundly impacted my life. It has taught me to let go of grudges, to see the humanity in others, and to cultivate compassion and empathy. It has allowed me to heal from past hurts and move forward with peace and freedom. In today's world, where conflict and division seem ever-present, forgiveness is more important than ever. It is a powerful tool that can heal wounds, bridge divides, and create a more compassionate and understanding society. My mother's lesson on forgiveness has become a guiding principle in my life. I strive to approach every situation with an open heart and a willingness to forgive. I have realised that forgiveness is not a sign of weakness but instead of strength and resilience.

As I navigate life's difficulties, I will always hold onto my mother's teachings on forgiveness. I am grateful for her unwavering wisdom and guidance, and I hope to pass on the valuable lesson of forgiveness to future generations.

My mother always used to say, "Nobody is perfect; we all make mistakes."

This simple yet profound statement has stayed with me throughout my life, shaping my perspective on myself and others. It underscores the reality that every single person is flawed and prone to error and that it is through our mistakes that we learn, grow, and become better individuals. Growing up, I learnt this lesson firsthand from my mother. She often reminded me that it was okay to make mistakes if I learnt from them and did better the next time. She would share her experiences of failures and setbacks, showing me that even the most robust and capable individuals are not immune to making mistakes.

This lesson of humility and self-acceptance has helped me navigate life's difficulties with grace and resilience. One of the most important things my mother taught me is owning up to my mistakes. Instead of trying to cover them up or shift the blame onto others, she encouraged me to take responsibility for my actions and the consequences that followed. This sense of accountability has helped me to earn the trust and respect of those around me, as they know that I am willing to admit when I am wrong and to make amends for it.

My mother also showed me that mistakes should not be feared or avoided but should be embraced as opportunities for growth and self-improvement. She would often say that it is through our mistakes that we learn valuable lessons about ourselves and the world around us. Instead of dwelling on our failures, we should use them as stepping stones towards success and personal development.

One of the most profound lessons I learnt from my mother is the importance of forgiveness towards others and oneself. She often reminded me that holding grudges and resentments only weighs us down and prevents us from moving forward. Instead, she encouraged me to let go of past mistakes and focus on the present moment, where we have the power to make positive choices and create a brighter future. In a world that often primarily values perfection and success, my mother's words remind us that our imperfections and mistakes are what make us human. We should not be ashamed of our failures but rather embrace them as opportunities for growth and self-discovery.

By acknowledging our flaws and learning from our mistakes, we can become more compassionate, understanding, and resilient. My mother's wise words have profoundly shaped my understanding of myself and others. She taught me that nobody is perfect and that it is through our mistakes that we learn, grow, and become better individuals. Through her guidance and example, I have seen the beauty in imperfection and the power of forgiveness. I am forever grateful for her wisdom and love, which continue to inspire me today.

My Mother Taught Me to Be Open to Criticism

Criticism can be challenging to accept. It can be painful, humbling, and difficult for our ego. However, my mother taught me that criticism is crucial for personal growth and development. She emphasised the importance of being open to feedback from friends, family, teachers, or mentors. She believed that criticism, when given constructively, can help us learn from our mistakes, improve our skills, and ultimately become better versions of ourselves. With her guidance and support, I could correct my mistakes, practice more effectively, and perform a piece confidently on the field. My mother's willingness to offer constructive criticism and guidance helped me become a better soccer player and, more importantly, a better person. As I grew older and entered the workforce, I encountered criticism in a different context. In my first job, I was eager to prove myself and excel.

However, I quickly learnt that success requires more than hard work and dedication. It also requires accepting feedback, learning from mistakes, and continuously improving. I remember a performance review with my manager, during which I received constructive criticism about my communication skills. Instead of becoming defensive or dismissive, I took my mother's advice to heart and listened carefully to the feedback. I asked for specific examples of where I could improve, sought advice on addressing my weaknesses, and implemented a plan to enhance my communication skills.

Over time, I noticed a significant improvement in my communication ability with colleagues, clients, and stakeholders. Thanks to the valuable feedback I received and acted upon, I became more confident, articulate, and persuasive in my interactions. My mother's lesson about being open to criticism has served me well in all areas of my life. It has helped me build stronger relationships, develop new skills, and overcome obstacles with resilience and determination. I have come to view criticism not as a threat but an opportunity for growth and self-discovery.

Reflecting on my journey and the lessons I have learnt from my mother, I am grateful for her unwavering support, guidance, and wisdom. She has been my most excellent teacher, shaping me into the person I am today and instilling in me the values of humility, perseverance, and lifelong learning. My mother's lesson about being open to criticism profoundly impacted my life. It taught me to embrace feedback, learn from my mistakes, and strive for continuous improvement. I am grateful for her guidance and support, which have helped me grow and thrive in my personal and professional pursuits. My mother will always be my most excellent teacher, and I will always be grateful for her invaluable lessons.

My Mother Taught Me the Importance of Clear Communication

Communication is a fundamental aspect of human interaction, enabling us to express our thoughts, feelings, and needs to others. We use various forms of communication, such as speaking, listening, writing, and gestures, to convey messages effectively. Communicating effectively is crucial for building strong relationships, resolving conflicts, and achieving success in both one's personal and professional spheres.

My mother has always emphasised the importance of communication in every aspect of my life, teaching me valuable lessons that have shaped my understanding and practice of effective communication. From an early age, my mother instilled in me the importance of listening actively and attentively when conversing with others. She often reminded me to listen to what others were saying, understand their perspectives and respond thoughtfully. By doing so, I learnt the significance of being present in conversations and showing respect to the speaker.

My mother also taught me the importance of asking questions and seeking clarification when necessary, encouraging me to engage in meaningful dialogue that fosters understanding and connection. In addition to listening, my mother stressed the importance of speaking clearly and concisely to convey my thoughts and ideas effectively. She taught me to organise my thoughts before speaking, to be mindful of my tone and body language, and to communicate confidently. Due to her guidance, I learnt the value of articulating my thoughts in a way that is easy for others to understand, fostering clarity and minimising misunderstandings.

Furthermore, my mother emphasised the importance of nonverbal communication, such as facial expressions, gestures, and body language, in conveying messages effectively. She taught me to be aware of my nonverbal cues and to pay attention to the nonverbal cues of others, as they can often reveal emotions and intentions that may not be expressed verbally. By understanding the power of nonverbal communication, I have learnt to communicate more effectively and to connect with others on a deeper level. My mother also taught me the importance of empathy and compassion in communication, encouraging me to consider the feelings and perspectives of others when engaging in conversations. She emphasised the value of active listening, validation, and support in building strong and meaningful relationships.

By practising empathy and compassion in my communication, I learnt to connect with others on a deeper level and to create a supportive and nurturing environment for open and honest dialogue. Through my mother's teachings, I have come to appreciate the transformative power of effective communication in all aspects of my life. I have learnt that communication is about exchanging words and connecting with others, fostering understanding, and building meaningful relationships. My mother's guidance has equipped me with the skills and mindset necessary to communicate confidently, empathetically, and effectively personally and professionally. Communication is a vital skill that plays a significant role in shaping our interactions with others and achieving success in various aspects of our lives.

My mother has been a constant source of guidance and inspiration in teaching me the importance of communication, emphasising the value of listening, speaking, nonverbal communication, empathy, and exhibiting compassion in building strong relationships and achieving mutual understanding. With her teachings in mind, I strive to communicate effectively, authentically, and compassionately in all my interactions, recognising the power of communication to create positive and meaningful connections with others.

My Mother Taught Me to Be Generous and Kind

My mother always emphasised the importance of generosity. From a young age, she taught me the value of giving back to others and helping those in need. Whether donating to charity, volunteering in our community, or simply being kind and compassionate towards others, my mother showed me that generosity was a virtue and a way of life.

One of my earliest memories of my mother teaching me about generosity was when I was about six years old. We were at the grocery store, and as we were checking out, the cashier accidentally gave my mother too much change. I remember my mother immediately pointing out the mistake and returning the extra money. I was initially confused, wondering why she would not keep it. But my mother explained that it was essential to be honest and fair, even if it meant giving something back that was not rightfully ours.

As I grew older, my mother continued to lead by example regarding generosity. She would always make extra food to share with our neighbours. She would help local community members at funerals, showing me firsthand how a small act of kindness could impact someone's life. I remember feeling inspired by her selflessness and compassion and wanting to follow her. My mother's teachings about generosity extended beyond just material possessions. She also taught me to be generous with my time and my emotions.

She showed me that a kind word or a listening ear could make a difference for someone struggling. I remember times when my mother would stop to help a stranger in need or would offer a shoulder to cry on to a friend going through a tough time. She taught me that generosity was not just about giving things but also about giving of yourself and your heart.

Reflecting on my mother's lessons about generosity, I realise that they have shaped me into who I am today. I approach every situation with a spirit of generosity, looking for ways to give back and positively impact those around me. Whether donating to a cause I believe in, volunteering in my community, or simply being there for a needy friend, I strive to embody my mother's values.

One of the most important lessons my mother taught me about generosity is that it is not about the size of the gesture but its intention. She showed me that even the most minor acts of kindness can have a ripple effect, spreading joy and compassion to others. Whether holding the door open for someone or offering a smile to a stranger, my mother taught me that generosity can be found in simple gestures.

My mother's generosity lessons remind me of the power of compassion and empathy in a world that sometimes feels cold and indifferent. She showed me that by being generous, we could make a difference in the lives of others and enrich our own lives in the process. Through her example, my mother taught me that true happiness comes not from what we have but from what we give.

As I continue my journey, I always carry my mother's teachings. I strive to be a beacon of generosity and kindness in a world that sometimes feels dark and chaotic. I remember her words, actions, and unwavering belief in the power of giving back, and I know that if I follow in her footsteps, I will always be on the right path.

Kindness is a virtue often overlooked in today's fast-paced and competitive world. However, it is one of the most essential qualities that a person can possess. My mother taught me the value of kindness from a young age, and it is a lesson that has stayed with me throughout my life. Growing up, my mother always helped others in need.

Whether volunteering at a local charity, donating to those less fortunate, or simply being there to listen to a friend in need, she always went out of her way to show kindness to others. I remember watching her in awe as she selflessly gave of herself to help those around her. It was through her actions that I learnt the true meaning of kindness. One of the most important lessons my mother taught me about kindness is that it does not have to be in the form of grand gestures or expensive gifts.

Kindness can be as simple as a smile, a kind word, or a helping hand. It is the little things that we do for others that can make the most significant impact. My mother showed me that kindness is about empathy, compassion, and understanding. It is about putting yourself in someone else's shoes and treating them with the same respect and dignity that you would want for yourself.

My mother's actions spoke louder than words when teaching me about kindness. She showed me that kindness is not just about how we treat others but also about how we treat ourselves. She taught me that it is essential to be kind, forgive ourselves for our mistakes, and treat ourselves with the same love and compassion we show others. By practising self-kindness, we can better show kindness to those around us. My mother's lessons in kindness have had a lasting impact on me. They have shaped the person I am today and influenced how I interact with others. I strive to always show kindness to those around me, whether a stranger on the street, a coworker in need, or a friend going through a difficult time.

Kindness is a powerful force that can bring people together, heal wounds, and create a more compassionate and understanding world. Today, it can be easy to get caught up in the hustle and bustle of everyday life and forget about the importance of kindness.

However, my mother's teachings have reminded me that kindness is a timeless and universal value that should be cherished and nurtured. It is a quality that can bring joy and happiness to both the giver and the receiver and can have a ripple effect that spreads kindness throughout the world.

Reflecting on my mother's lessons about kindness, I am grateful for her wisdom and guidance. She has shown me that kindness is a choice that we make every day and that it can have a profound impact on the world around us. I am forever grateful for the love and kindness my mother has shown me, and I will continue to strive to live my life in a way that honours the values she instilled in me.

My Mother Taught Me to Trust My Inner Voice

My mother has always been my most excellent teacher. From a young age, she instilled in me the importance of listening to my inner voice. She taught me that our intuition can be a powerful guide in navigating life's challenges and making important decisions. Reflecting on the lessons she has imparted, I am grateful for the wisdom she shared and its impact on my life. One of the most valuable lessons my mother taught me is the importance of trusting my instincts. She would often say, "Listen to that voice inside you. It knows what is best for you." At first, I did not fully understand what she meant. How could a voice inside me know more than my rational mind? But as I grew older and faced more complex decisions, I began to see the truth of her words.

One instance stands out in my memory. I was in high school and struggling with choosing a college to attend. I visited several campuses, researched different programmes, and sought advice from friends and family. Yet, I found myself feeling uncertain and overwhelmed. I turned to my mother for guidance, and she said, "Close your eyes, take a deep breath, and listen to your heart. It will lead you in the right direction." I followed her advice and meditated, quieting my mind and tuning into my inner voice. As I did so, a sense of clarity washed over me. I realised that the college I had initially dismissed as too far from home was the best fit for me. It offered the programmes I was most interested in, had a supportive community, and felt like a place where I could grow and thrive. With my mother's encouragement, I chose to attend that college, which was one of the best decisions I had ever made. I made lifelong friends and discovered new passions. Looking back, I am grateful for my mother's guidance and for teaching me to trust my instincts.

Another lesson my mother taught me is the importance of self-care. She often reminded me that we cannot truly listen to our inner voice if constantly stressed, exhausted, or overwhelmed. She encouraged me to take time for myself, whether it was through meditation, exercise, or simply spending time in nature. I remember a time when I was juggling multiple responsibilities – school, work, extracurricular activities – and was feeling burnt out. My mother noticed my struggles and sat me down for a heart-to-heart conversation. She said, "Listen to your body. It is telling you that you need rest and to recharge. Do not ignore those signs."

Her words struck a chord with me, and I realised I had been neglecting my well-being in pursuit of achievement. I took her advice to heart and made a conscious effort to prioritise self-care. I started practising yoga, going for walks in the park, and setting aside time for relaxation. As I did so, I found that my inner voice became more precise and decisive. I could make choices that aligned with my values and brought me joy.

My mother's teachings on listening to my inner voice profoundly impacted my life. They helped me navigate challenging situations, make important decisions, and stay true to myself. I am forever grateful for her wisdom, guidance, and unconditional love. My mother taught me the invaluable lesson of listening to my inner voice. Her guidance taught me to trust my instincts, prioritise self-care, and follow the right path. I carry her teachings with me as I navigate life's journey, knowing that her voice will always guide me.

My Mother Taught Me to Work Hard and to Be Committed

My mother constantly reminded me that nothing comes for free and that if I wanted to achieve my goals, I would have to put in the effort and dedication to make it happen. Growing up, my mother always led by example. She worked long hours to provide for our family and never complained about the sacrifices she had to make. Despite her challenges, she never gave up and always pushed through with a tireless determination that inspired me to do the same. One of the most important lessons my mother taught me was the importance of setting goals and working towards them with unwavering commitment. She often said, "If you want something, you must go after it with all your heart. Success does not just come knocking on your door - you must actively pursue it." This lesson has stuck with me throughout my life and guided me in pursuing my dreams. Whether getting into a competitive university, landing a job at a prestigious company, or pursuing my passion for writing, I have always approached my goals with purpose and determination, thanks to my mother's wise words.

My mother also emphasised the value of hard work and perseverance. She would often say, "Nothing worth having comes easy. If you want something, you have to be willing to work for it." This simple yet powerful message has been a driving force in my life, driving me to push through obstacles and never give up, no matter how challenging the road. My mother's teachings have shaped me into the person I am today - someone who is not afraid to roll up their sleeves and work hard to achieve their goals. I have carried her lessons into every aspect of my life, from my career to my relationships. I have learnt that success is not a result of luck or chance but rather a product of dedication, perseverance, and hard work.

My Mother's Concern Over My Upbringing

My mother has always been concerned about my growth and development, both physically and emotionally. She is always looking out for my well-being and ensuring that I am on the right path towards becoming a successful and happy individual. Her concerns stem from her deep love and care for me and her desire to see me thrive in all aspects of my life. My physical health is one of my mother's main concerns about my growth. She always reminds me to eat well, exercise regularly, and get enough rest. She knows a healthy body is essential for a healthy mind and wants to ensure I care for myself properly. My mother often cooks nutritious meals for me and encourages me to stay active by participating in sports or walking. She also ensures that I go for regular check-ups at the doctor to monitor my growth and development.

My mother was also concerned about my emotional well-being. She wanted me to be confident, resilient, and able to handle the challenges that life might throw at me. My mother gave me a listening ear whenever I was feeling down or stressed, and she offered me guidance and support to help me navigate through difficult situations. She encouraged me to be open and honest about my feelings and taught me the importance of self-care and self-love.

My mother was concerned about another aspect of my growth: my education. She wanted me to excel academically and make the most of my potential. My mother constantly supported me in my studies, helping me with homework, projects, and exam preparations. She instilled in me the value of hard work and determination and motivated me to strive for excellence in all I did. My mother also advocated for my education by communicating with my teachers and school administrators to ensure I received the necessary support and resources to succeed.

Furthermore, my mother was concerned about my social development. She wants me to be kind, respectful, and empathetic towards others. My mother taught me the importance of treating others with kindness and compassion, and she encouraged me to make friends, build relationships, and collaborate with others. She believes that social skills are essential for success in both personal and professional life, and she guided me in developing healthy social interactions and communication skills. My mother's concerns about my growth were driven by her unconditional love and devotion towards me. She wants the best for me and always seeks my well-being.

Growing up in a community where alcohol and drugs are prevalent can have a significant impact on a child's upbringing. As a result, parents often worry about the influences their children are exposed to and try to protect them from the negative consequences of substance abuse. My mother always been concerned about my upbringing and the of alcohol and drugs in our community. From a young age, my mother instilled in me the importance of making good choices and staying away from harmful substances. She explained to me the consequences of alcohol and drug abuse, such as addiction, health problems, and legal troubles. She also shared with me personal stories of people she knew who had struggled with addiction and the impact it had on their lives and families.

Despite my mother's warnings, I witnessed firsthand the prevalence of alcohol and drug use in our community. I saw friends and classmates experimenting with substances, and I felt the pressure to join in despite knowing the potential risks. In these moments, my mother's concern became even more evident as she reminded me of the importance of staying true to myself and resisting the urge to follow the crowd. My mother's concern for my upbringing and the risks of alcohol and drugs in our community only intensified as I entered my teenage years. She became more vigilant in monitoring my activities and those I associated with. She set strict rules and boundaries to ensure that I stayed away from situations that could lead to experimentation with substances. While I sometimes resented her restrictions, I now realise they were meant to protect me and help me make informed decisions. As I reflect on my upbringing and my mother's concern about alcohol and drugs in our community, I am grateful for her unwavering support and guidance. Her constant reminders to stay true to myself and make responsible choices have shaped the person I am today. I have learnt to prioritise my well-being and surround myself with positive influences, even in the face of peer pressure and societal norms.

As I grew older, my mother continued to express her concerns about the temptations of alcohol and drugs in our community. She warned me about peer pressure and the dangers of trying to fit in by engaging in risky behaviours. She encouraged me to surround myself with positive influences and make decisions aligning with my values and goals. Her advice, guidance, and support have been instrumental in shaping me into the person I am today, and I am forever grateful for her unwavering care and concern.

My Mother Taught Me the Value of Respect

Respect is a fundamental value that is the foundation for healthy and fulfilling relationships. It is the acknowledgement of the worth and dignity of others, recognising their rights, thoughts, and feelings. My mother has always been a strong advocate for respect, instilling this value in me from a young age. Her words and actions taught me the importance of treating others with kindness, empathy, and consideration. Growing up, my mother always emphasised the golden rule - treating others as you would like them to treat you. She taught me that respect is not just a mere formality but also a way of showing appreciation for individuals' unique qualities and experiences. Whether it was interacting with classmates, siblings, or elders, my mother reminded me to be mindful of the impact of my words and actions on others. She often said, "You may not agree with someone's opinions or actions, but you can still show them respect as a fellow human being."

One of the most potent lessons my mother taught me about respect was through her behaviour. She treated everyone she met with kindness and dignity, regardless of their social status or background. She showed me that respect knows no boundaries and that every person deserves to be treated with decency and fairness. My mother's teachings about respect extended beyond just interpersonal relationships. She also emphasised the importance of respecting oneself - setting boundaries, standing up for one's beliefs, and practising self-care. She often reminded me that self-respect is the foundation for healthy self-esteem and resilience in adversity. I learnt that valuing and honouring myself could help me better navigate life's challenges while staying true to my values and principles.

One of the most impactful lessons my mother taught me about respect was during a difficult time in our family. My parents were going through a rough patch in their marriage, and tensions were high at home. Despite the turmoil and emotional strain, my mother always maintained her composure and treated my father respectfully and with dignity. She never resorted to insults or belittling remarks, communicating calmly and assertively. Through her actions, she showed me that respect is not just reserved for those we admire or agree with but also for those with whom we may have disagreements or conflicts. Reflecting on my mother's teachings about respect, I realise how profoundly they have shaped my values and behaviours. I strive to emulate her example by treating others with kindness, empathy, and understanding. I also consciously try to practise self-respect, set boundaries, and honour my needs and values.

In today's fast-paced and often chaotic world, respect is more important than ever. Respect serves as a bridge between individuals, fostering understanding, empathy, and cooperation. It is the foundation for healthy relationships, effective communication, and a harmonious society. By teaching me respect, my mother gave me a powerful tool that guided my interactions and decisions personally and professionally.

My mother's teachings about respect profoundly impacted my life. Her words and actions taught me the importance of treating others with kindness, empathy, and consideration. She showed me that respect was not just a mere formality but a way of honouring the worth and dignity of every individual. I am grateful for the valuable lessons my mother taught me about respect, and I strive to embody this value in all aspects of my life.

My Mother Taught Me the Value of Responsibility, Trust and Accountability

As I reflect on my upbringing and the values instilled in me by my, one lesson stands out above all others - the importance of taking responsibility for my actions. This valuable lesson was not taught to me through lectures or admonishments but rather through the daily example set by my mother. From a young age, I witnessed how my mother took ownership of her good and bad decisions and always sought to learn and grow from her mistakes. This powerful example has had a lasting impact on me and has shaped the person I am today.

My mother believed that to mature and grow, I needed to take responsibility for my actions and their outcomes. That mindset was ingrained in me from a young age and has become a guiding principle in my life. As I grew older and faced more complex challenges, the lesson of taking responsibility for my actions became even more crucial.

In college, I encountered situations that tested my integrity and decision-making abilities. Whether resisting the temptation to plagiarise a paper or owning up to a mistake at work, I always remembered the importance of being accountable for my actions. Through these experiences, I realised that taking responsibility for my actions is not just about admitting when I am wrong but also about actively seeking ways to make amends and learn from my mistakes. It is about recognising the impact of my decisions on others and striving to act with integrity and honesty in all aspects of my life.

Trust is a fundamental pillar of any relationship with family, friends, or colleagues. Relationships can easily crumble without trust, leading to feelings of betrayal, insecurity, and hate. Trust is earned over time through consistent actions and behaviours that demonstrate reliability, honesty, and integrity.

My understanding and appreciation of trust were shaped and nurtured by my mother, who exemplified the true meaning of trust through her actions as a church treasurer. Growing up, my mother served as the treasurer of our local church. This role required her to manage the church's finances, including collecting donations, keeping records, and making financial decisions to ensure the church's economic health. As a young child, I did not fully grasp the importance of her role, but as I grew older, I began to understand the immense responsibility and trust placed in her hands. One of the most remarkable things about my mother's tenure as the church treasurer was her unwavering commitment to honesty and integrity. Despite having access to the church's funds, my mother never once took a cent for herself. She ensured that every donation was recorded correctly and accounted for and that the church's finances were handled with the utmost care and transparency.

This level of honesty and integrity was a job requirement for my mother and a way of life. My mother's actions taught me the value of trust tangibly and profoundly. By consistently demonstrating honesty and integrity in her role as the church treasurer, she showed me that trust was not just about words or promises – it was about actions and behaviours. Trust is earned through hard work, dedication, and a commitment to doing the right thing, even when no one is watching.

My mother taught me the importance of accountability and responsibility through her actions. As the church treasurer, she understood she was accountable to the church community and a higher power. She took her role seriously and ensured that every financial decision was in the church's best interest and mission. This level of accountability and responsibility inspired me to take ownership of my actions and always strive to do the right thing, even when difficult or unpopular. My mother's example impacted me and shaped how I approached relationships and responsibilities. Trust is a precious commodity that must be earned and cherished. It should never be taken for granted but rather nurtured and protected through consistent actions and behaviours that demonstrate honesty, integrity, and reliability. **My mother's unwavering commitment to trust was a beacon of light and inspiration in a world where trust is often fragile and easily broken.** Her actions as a church treasurer showed me the true meaning of trust and instilled a deep appreciation for the value of honesty, integrity, and accountability. I am grateful for the lessons she has taught me, and I strive to live my life honouring her legacy of trust and integrity.

My Mother Taught Me the Value of Commitment

Commitment is a virtue that is sometimes difficult to uphold, especially when one is faced with challenges and difficulties. However, my mother has been a shining example of unwavering commitment in my life, particularly during turmoil and uncertainty in her marriage. Growing up, my parents' marriage seemed perfect to me. They were always laughing, hugging, and showing affection toward each other. It was the kind of love that I aspired to find one day for myself. However, as I grew older, I noticed cracks in their relationship.

There were more arguments, less laughter, and an undeniable tension lingered.

I watched as my mother struggled to navigate the rough waters of a failing marriage. Despite her challenges, she never wavered in her commitment to my father and our family. She dedicated herself to working things out, seeking counselling, and trying her best to salvage what they had built together over the years. It was not an easy journey, and there were many times when she could have given up and walked away. But she chose to stay and to fight for the love that she believed in. Through her actions, my mother taught me the value of commitment. She showed me that commitment is not just about the good times and the easy moments but is also about persevering through the tough times and the struggles. It is about staying faithful to your promises and obligations, even when it would be easier to walk away.

My mother's commitment to her marriage taught me that love is not always perfect but is worth fighting for. I saw the sacrifices that my mother made to keep her commitment intact. She put her own needs and desires aside to focus on the well-being of her family. She swallowed her pride and ego to compromise and find common ground with my father. She showed me that commitment requires selflessness and a willingness to put others before yourself. There were moments when I questioned why my mother stayed in a marriage that seemed to be falling apart. I wondered if it would have been easier for her to walk away and start anew. But as I grew older, I began to understand the depth of her commitment. I saw the love that she still had for my father, the history that they shared, and the family that they had built together. I realised that commitment is not just about staying together for the sake of appearances but is also about honouring the bond you have created with another person. My mother's commitment to her marriage also taught me the importance of resilience and perseverance. She faced insurmountable obstacles and challenges, but she never gave up. She continued working on her relationship, communicating openly and honestly, and seeking help when needed.

She showed me that commitment is not a one-time decision but a daily choice that requires effort, patience, and determination.

Through my mother's example, I have learnt to value commitment in all aspects of my life. Whether in my relationships, career, or personal goals, I understand the importance of staying true to my commitments and never giving up when faced with difficulties. I have seen firsthand the power of commitment to transform and strengthen a bond, and I strive to embody that same level of dedication in my own life. My mother's unwavering commitment to her marriage has been a profound lesson for me. She showed me the true meaning of dedication, resilience, and selflessness. Through her actions, I learnt that commitment is a cornerstone of any successful relationship and requires effort, sacrifice, and a steadfast belief in the value of love. I am grateful for the example my mother set for me, and I hope to carry forward her legacy of commitment in my own life.

My Mother Taught Me the Value of Honesty and Humility

Honesty is a moral value that holds great importance in one's life. It is the foundation upon which trust, and relationships are built. Throughout my life, my mother was a shining example of the value of honesty. She taught me that being honest not only benefits yourself but that it also benefits those around you. From a young age, my mother instilled in me the importance of always telling the truth. She would always say, "Honesty is the best policy." At first, I did not fully understand how being honest could impact my life, but as I grew older, I began to see the truth of her words.

One of the most important lessons my mother taught me about honesty is that it builds trust. When you are honest with others, they are more likely to trust and rely on you. This trust forms the foundation of solid relationships, whether it be with friends, family, or coworkers. Trust can easily be broken without honesty, leading to strained relationships and a sense of betrayal. I remember when I was tempted to lie to my friend about a mistake I had made. I was afraid of how she would react if she knew the truth. However, my mother encouraged me to be honest and face the consequences of my actions. Although challenging, I took her advice and told my friend the truth. To my surprise, she appreciated my honesty, and we were able to work through the issue together. This experience taught me that honesty can lead to more robust and meaningful relationships, even though it may be challenging. Another lesson my mother taught me about honesty was that it builds character. When you are honest, you show integrity and strength of character. People respect honest people, which can lead to opportunities and success. Conversely, lying can damage your reputation and credibility.

My mother always told me, "It is better to be known as an honest person than a liar." I have seen firsthand how my mother's honesty positively impacted her life. She is respected by her peers and loved by her family because of her unwavering commitment to the truth. Her honesty not only shaped the person she is today, but it also influenced those around her, including me. I strive to live with the same honesty and integrity my mother demonstrated. Being honest might not always be easy, but the benefits outweigh the consequences. I have experienced the positive effects of honesty on relationships, trust, and personal growth. Honesty is a value that holds great significance in one's life. My mother has been a guiding light in teaching me the importance of honesty. Through her example, I learnt that honesty builds trust, strengthens relationships, and shapes character. I am grateful for the lessons my mother taught me, and I will continue to live my life with honesty and integrity.

Humility is a virtue that is often overlooked today. In a world that values success, wealth, and status, humility is usually seen as a weakness. However, from a young age, my mother taught me the value of humility and showed how it could shape a person's character and lead to greater personal fulfilment.

Growing up, my mother always emphasised the importance of humility and treating others with kindness and respect. She often reminded me that I had to remain grounded and always maintain my values no matter how successful or accomplished I may become. She would share stories of great leaders and thinkers who possessed humility and how it contributed to their success and impact on the world.

One story my mother often shared with me was about Nelson Mandela, the leader of the African National Congress. Despite his significant influence and power, Mandela remained humble and committed to serving others. He lived a simple life, wore humble clothing, and dedicated his life to the betterment of others.

Through my mother's teachings and examples, I learnt that humility was not about thinking less of oneself but of thinking of oneself less. It is about putting others before oneself, acknowledging one's imperfections, and being open to learning from others. My mother often told me that humility is a sign of strength, not weakness, as it requires self-awareness and a willingness to grow and change. In my own life, I have seen the power of humility in action. When I approach challenges with a humble mindset, I am more open to feedback and constructive criticism. I am willing to admit I am wrong and can learn from my mistakes. I can put my ego aside and collaborate to achieve more significant outcomes. Humility has helped me build stronger relationships, navigate challenging situations, and approach life with gratitude and more perspective.

One of the most profound lessons my mother taught me about humility is the importance of serving others. She often volunteered her time and resources to help those in need, whether donating to charities, volunteering at local community events, or simply lending a listening ear to a friend in need. My mother's acts of kindness and service taught me that true humility is not just about how we carry ourselves but also how we treat others. Maintaining a humble attitude can be challenging in a society that often rewards self-promotion and individualism. However, my mother's teachings showed me humility is a timeless virtue that transcends social expectations and personal achievements. It is a quality that can enrich one's life, foster deeper connections with others, and lead to a greater sense of purpose and fulfilment. Reflecting on my mother's lessons about humility, I am reminded of its profound impact on my life. I strive to embody humility in everyday interactions, to approach challenges with an open mind and a humble heart, and always to seek ways to serve others. My mother's wisdom and example inspire me to lead a life of humility, compassion, and gratitude.

My mother imparted the value of humility, a lesson I will carry with me throughout my life. Through her teachings and examples, I learnt that humility is a powerful virtue that can shape one's character, influence relationships, and guide one towards more incredible personal growth and fulfilment. My mother's wisdom and guidance have shown me that humility is not just a trait to be admired but a quality to be embraced and lived out in every aspect of life.

My Family Traditions

Growing up in a family that strongly believed in traditional values and customs dramatically shaped my perspective on life and the world around me. From a young age, I was taught the importance of honouring our ancestors, following cultural traditions and maintaining strong family unity. These values have influenced every aspect of my life, from how I interact with others to my daily choices. My father's side of the family has always been deeply rooted in tradition, with a strong emphasis on preserving the customs and practices of our ancestors. Every aspect of our lives is steeped in tradition and ritual, from the foods we eat to how we celebrate holidays. I was taught from a young age that these practices are not simply old-fashioned ways of doing things but essential links to our past that connect us to our cultural heritage.

One of the most important traditions in my family is the practice of honouring our ancestors. Our ancestors always watch over and guide us from the spirit world, so showing them respect and gratitude is essential. We regularly visit the graves of our ancestors, leaving offerings of food, flowers, and incense to pay our respects. This practice taught me the importance of remembering where I come from and honouring those who came before me. In addition to honouring our ancestors, my family also strongly emphasises following cultural traditions in our daily lives. This includes everything from how we dress to how we celebrate holidays. For example, we wear traditional clothing during important family events and gatherings, such as weddings and festivals. These customs are not just for show but are meaningful symbols of our cultural identity and heritage.

One of the most cherished traditions in my family is the celebration of the New Year. This holiday is a time to unite as a family, share meals, and exchange gifts. We follow strict rituals during this time, such as cleaning the house to sweep away bad luck and preparing unique dishes that are believed to bring good fortune in the new year. These traditions have been passed down through generations and are essential to our family's identity. Growing up in a family that values tradition taught me the importance of family unity.

Family is vital; we must always support and care for one another. This unity is evident in how we come together to celebrate special occasions, lend a helping hand in times of need, and make decisions as a collective group. This strong sense of family unity has instilled in me a deep respect for my relatives and a commitment to always putting family first.

Despite the many benefits of growing up in a traditional family, some challenges come with it. It can be difficult to balance the expectations of tradition with the pressures of modern society. For example, there have been times when I have felt torn between following my family's customs and traditions and pursuing my own goals and values. However, I have realised that tradition does not have to be at odds with modernity – honouring our past while embracing the future is possible. Growing up in a family that strongly values tradition has profoundly impacted my life. From honouring our ancestors to following cultural customs, these traditions shaped my identity. While there were challenges, I am grateful for the deep sense of cultural identity and family unity instilled in me. I will continue to carry these values as I navigate through life, always remembering the importance of tradition and its power to connect us to our past and shape our future.

My Mother and God

The Bible is a sacred text that holds immense importance for Christians worldwide. It contains teachings, stories, and wisdom passed down through generations, guiding believers on their spiritual journey. One particularly important verse in the Bible is when Jesus tells his disciples to allow the children to come to him. This passage can be found in the book of Matthew, chapter 19, verse 14, which reads, "Let the little children come to me, and do not hinder them, for the kingdom of heaven belongs to such as these." This verse is rich in symbolism and meaning.

One of the first things that strikes us about this verse is the image of Jesus welcoming children with open arms. In the society of Jesus' time, children were often seen as insignificant and of little value. They should have been given more attention or importance, especially in religious circles.

By inviting the children to come to him, Jesus challenged the prevailing attitudes of the day and reminded his disciples that everyone, regardless of age or status, is worthy of God's love and grace. This act of Jesus also highlighted the importance of innocence and purity in the eyes of God. Children are often seen as symbols of innocence and simplicity, qualities that Jesus values highly. In their guilelessness and lack of pretence, children can approach God with a pure heart and genuine trust. Jesus' words serve as a reminder to his disciples that to enter the kingdom of heaven, one must possess the same childlike faith and humility.

Furthermore, Jesus' command to allow the children to come to him emphasises the inclusive nature of his ministry. Throughout his teachings, Jesus consistently reached out to those on the margins – the poor, the sick, and the outcasts. By welcoming the children, he again demonstrates his compassion and concern for society's marginalised and vulnerable members. His message is clear: everyone is welcome in the kingdom of God, regardless of their social status or background. Additionally, this verse serves as a powerful reminder of the importance of nurturing and protecting the most vulnerable members of society.

Children are often most in need of care, love, and guidance. By instructing his disciples to allow the children to come to him, Jesus is highlighting the need for adults to take responsibility for the well-being and spiritual development of the younger generation. This message is particularly relevant today, where children are often overlooked or neglected, and their voices are not always heard or valued. In a broader sense, this verse also speaks to humility and dependence on God. Children depend on adults for care and protection, just as we rely on God for our salvation and sustenance.

By encouraging his disciples to allow the children to come to him, Jesus reminds us of our need to approach God with a humble and trusting heart, like a child. This message is a powerful reminder of our reliance on God's grace and mercy in a world that often values self-sufficiency and independence. The Bible verse where Jesus tells his disciples to allow the children to come to him is a profound and meaningful passage that carries timeless truths and lessons for believers. It challenges social norms, celebrates innocence and humility, and demonstrates God's inclusive love for all. This verse serves as a reminder of the importance of caring for the most vulnerable members of society, nurturing a childlike faith and trust in God, and embodying humility and dependence on God. As Christians, we are called to embody these values in our lives and welcome all, especially the children, into the kingdom of God.

As a woman of faith, my mother always instilled in us the importance of trust in God's plan. She taught us about God and His ways from a young age, guiding us on the path of righteousness and encouraging us to live according to His will. Growing up in a household where faith and spirituality were central to our lives, my siblings and I were raised with a deep understanding of the importance of God in our lives. My mother taught us the power of prayer, the importance of attending church regularly, and the significance of living a life guided by love, compassion, and forgiveness. One of the critical lessons my mother taught us was the importance of trusting in God's plan for our lives. She reminded us that even in times of hardship and struggle, God was always there to guide us and provide us with strength and comfort. Through her words and actions, my mother showed us that faith is a powerful force that can help us navigate life's challenges and find peace and solace in times of need.

My mother also emphasised the importance of living a life of integrity and righteousness. She taught us to always treat others with kindness and respect, to be honest and truthful in all our dealings, and to strive to be pleasing to God. By setting a positive example for us to follow, my mother instilled in us the values of humility, compassion, and selflessness, guiding us toward spiritual growth and personal development. In addition to teaching us about God and His ways, my mother encouraged us to deepen our understanding of our faith through study and reflection. She often read the Bible with us, discussing its teachings and helping us apply them. Through these conversations, my mother helped us develop a deeper connection to our faith and a greater appreciation for the wisdom and guidance in the scriptures.

As a God-fearing woman, my mother also taught us the importance of service and giving back to others. She showed us that true faith is not just about personal holiness but also about reaching out to those in need and positively impacting the world.

Through her teachings and example, my mother instilled in us a deep gratitude and appreciation for all we have been blessed with. She reminded us that our faith should provide comfort and strength for ourselves and hope and inspiration for others. By living a life of faith and service, my mother showed us that we could make a difference in the world and bring glory to God through our actions and deeds.

As a God-fearing woman, my mother played a pivotal role in shaping our understanding of faith, spirituality, and the importance of living a life guided by God's teachings. Her words, actions, and example taught us the value of trust, integrity, and service, guiding us toward spiritual growth and personal development. I am grateful for the lessons my mother taught me about God and His ways, and I strive to live my life in a way that honours her teachings and brings glory to the God we both worship.

My Mother Taught Me How to Pray

I was taught from a very young age the importance of prayer. My mother instilled in me the habit of praying daily and seeking guidance from God in everything I do. As a child, I would sit with my mother every evening before bed, and we would recite prayers together. These moments were special to me as they brought me closer to God and strengthened the bond between my mother and me. As I grew older, the concept of prayer became more profound and meaningful to me. I began to understand the power of prayer in shaping my life and the lives of those around me. My mother always emphasised the importance of praying sincerely and believing God would answer our prayers in His time and His way. This belief gave me hope and comfort in times of trials and tribulations.

One of the most important lessons my mother taught me about prayer was the need for gratitude. She always reminded me to thank God for His blessings and answered prayers, no matter how big or small they might seem. Gratitude, she said, opens the doors to even more blessings and divine favours. This simple yet profound lesson has stayed with me throughout my life and shaped my attitude towards prayer and life.

Prayer is not just a ritual or a duty but a form of communication and connection with the divine. It is a way to express my deepest desires, fears, hopes, and dreams to God. It is a way for me to seek guidance, solace, and strength in times of need. It is a way to surrender my will to the divine will and trust that God knows what is best for me. My mother's teachings on prayer have profoundly impacted me and helped me navigate various life challenges and obstacles. Whenever I feel lost or confused, I turn to prayer as a source of guidance and comfort.

Prayer has become a constant companion and a source of strength for me, especially during difficult times. Prayer has also taught me humility and patience. It has taught me to trust in God's timing and to surrender to His will, even when things do not go as planned. Through prayer, I have learnt to accept that not everything is within my control and that I must have faith in God's plan. Moreover, prayer has taught me the importance of compassion and empathy towards others. As I pray for my own needs and desires, I am reminded to pray for the well-being and happiness of others as well. Prayer has helped me cultivate a sense of interconnectedness and unity with all living beings, as we are all children of God seeking His divine grace and mercy.

Prayer is a religious practice and a way of life for me. It is a source of comfort, guidance, and strength instilled in me by my God-fearing mother. Through prayer, I have learnt to trust in God's plan, to be grateful for His blessings, and to seek His guidance in all aspects of my life. As a God-fearing person, I will continue to uphold the practice of prayer and pass on this invaluable lesson to future generations. Prayer is a powerful tool that can transform lives and bring us closer to the divine presence of God.

A Child Can Make a Big Mistake by Not Listening to Their Mother

The bond between a mother and child is one of the most vital relationships in a person's life. Mothers play a critical role in shaping their children's character, values, and behaviour. However, as children grow and develop, they may struggle to listen to and respect their mothers. This can be a detrimental mistake, as not listening and respecting one's mother can negatively affect a child's overall well-being and future success.

One of the biggest mistakes a child can make is not listening to and respecting his mother. Mothers often provide their children with love, care, and guidance from a young age. They teach children the difference between right and wrong, help children navigate challenging situations, and provide a sense of security and stability. When a child refuses to listen to or respect their mother, they are essentially rejecting the wisdom and guidance they have to offer. This can lead to a breakdown in communication and trust between the child and their mother, ultimately causing strain on their relationship. Not listening to and respecting one's mother can also harm a child's development and behaviour.

Mothers play a significant role in shaping their children's character and values. When a child disregards his mother's guidance and advice, he may be more vulnerable to making poor decisions and engaging in risky behaviours. This can lead to negative consequences such as academic struggles, relationship issues, and even involvement in criminal activities.

By not listening to and respecting his mother, a child is missing out on an essential source of support and guidance to help him navigate life's challenges and make better choices. Furthermore, not listening to and respecting one's mother can have long-term effects on a child's mental and emotional well-being.

Mothers are usually the ones who provide emotional support and encouragement for their children. When a child rejects their mother's efforts to offer comfort and reassurance, he may struggle to cope with stress, anxiety, and other emotional challenges. This can lead to feelings of isolation, loneliness, and low self-esteem. Overall, not listening to and respecting his mother can damage a child's mental health and overall happiness.

Additionally, not listening to and respecting one's mother can negatively affect a child's future success and relationships. Mothers often instil essential values such as respect, responsibility, and empathy in their children. When a child fails to listen to and respect his mother, they may struggle to develop these essential qualities. This can hinder their ability to build meaningful relationships, excel in school or work, and lead fulfilling and successful lives.

Not listening to and respecting one's mother is a significant mistake that can have far-reaching consequences for a child's well-being and future. Mothers play a crucial role in shaping their children's character, values, and behaviour. When a child refuses to listen to and respect his mother, he jeopardises their relationship and lacks essential guidance and support to help him navigate life's challenges. Children must recognise the importance of listening to and respecting their mothers to cultivate a strong bond, develop positive character traits, and succeed.

In Xhosa culture, the relationship between a mother and her son is deeply rooted in tradition and respect. As a son, my responsibility towards my mother is significant in the Xhosa community. It is believed that the bond between a mother and her child is sacred and should be cherished and always honoured.

One of my primary responsibilities towards my mother as a son is to show her love and respect. In Xhosa culture, the mother is considered the primary caregiver and nurturer of the family. She sacrifices her own needs and desires to take care of her children. As a son, I must show appreciation for all my mother has done for me by treating her with love and kindness.

I am also responsible for providing for my mother in any way possible. In Xhosa culture, the son is expected to care for his mother as she grows older and may need assistance with daily tasks. This could include financial support, helping with household chores, or simply being there for her when she needs someone to talk to. By fulfilling this responsibility, I am showing my mother that I value her well-being and want to ensure that she has a comfortable and happy life.

In addition to providing for my mother, I must also uphold the values and traditions of our Xhosa culture. This includes participating in important rituals and ceremonies honouring our ancestors and strengthening our community bonds. As a son, I am responsible for passing down these traditions to future generations and ensuring that our cultural heritage continues to thrive.

Furthermore, I must uphold the principles of Ubuntu, which are central to Xhosa culture. Ubuntu is the belief in the interconnectedness of all people and the importance of treating others with kindness and compassion. As a son, I must embody these principles in my interactions with my mother and others in my community. By showing empathy and understanding towards my mother, I am demonstrating my commitment to upholding the values of Ubuntu. I also need to communicate openly and honestly with my mother. In Xhosa culture, communication is critical to maintaining strong family relationships. As a son, I must be willing to listen to my mother's advice and guidance and to share my thoughts and feelings with her. By fostering open communication, I can strengthen the bond between us and ensure that we have a healthy and supportive relationship.

As a son of Xhosa culture, my responsibility towards my mother is multifaceted and deeply rooted in tradition. I must show her love and respect, provide for her needs, uphold our cultural values and traditions, embody the principles of Ubuntu, and communicate openly and honestly. By fulfilling these responsibilities, I can honour my mother and our Xhosa heritage and contribute to the well-being of our family and community.

Inheriting the Promises of God

On November 7, 2013, a day that will forever be etched in my memory, my mother called my family and me to the living room. As we gathered around, she had a solemn look that conveyed a sense of importance and gravitas. Little did I know that this day would mark a turning point in my life, as my mother would give us something of immense value and significance.

As my mother stood before us, she held her hands, clasping a small, worn-out book. It was a Bible that had seen years of use and had been a constant companion to her. She spoke softly with tears in her eyes, "This is all I am and have. It is my gift from the bottom of my heart." At that moment, I was overcome with a mixture of emotions - gratitude, love, and a sense of responsibility.

The Bible my mother had gifted us was more than just a book; it symbolised her faith, values, and legacy. It was a tangible representation of her love for us, her desire for us to find solace and guidance in its pages. Holding the Bible in my hands, I could not help but feel a sense of awe and reverence. This small book held within its pages the wisdom of centuries, the stories of faith and redemption, and the teachings of love and compassion. It was a treasure trove of knowledge and inspiration, a guide for navigating life's challenges and triumphs. I increasingly turned to the Bible in the following days and weeks. I would read its verses in times of doubt and uncertainty, seeking comfort and guidance in its timeless words. I would meditate on its teachings, reflecting on the lessons of humility, forgiveness, and perseverance. My mother's gift of the Bible became a touchstone for me, a source of strength and solace in moments of darkness. Its words gave me a sense of purpose and direction, inspiring me to live a life of integrity and compassion. I was drawn to its stories of faith and courage, finding echoes of my struggles and triumphs in its pages.

As I delved deeper into the Bible, I discovered a newfound connection to my mother. I realised that her gift was not just a physical object but a symbol of her enduring love and faith. It reminded me of the values she had instilled in me through her actions and words, the lessons of kindness, empathy, and generosity. In a world filled with worldly pursuits and fleeting pleasures, my mother's gift of the Bible was a poignant reminder of what truly matters in life.

It was a reminder to cherish family bonds, uphold the values of faith and love, and seek solace in the wisdom of the ages. Looking back on that fateful day in November 2013, I am grateful for the gift my mother bestowed upon me. Her simple passing down of her cherished Bible has profoundly impacted my life, shaping my values, beliefs, and actions. It is a legacy I will always carry, a reminder of the enduring power of love and faith. As I continue my life's journey, I know that the gift of the Bible from my mother will be my constant companion. Its pages will be a beacon of light in times of darkness, a source of comfort in times of distress, and a wellspring of wisdom in times of confusion. I am eternally grateful for this precious gift, given from the bottom of her heart, and I will strive to honour it by living a life of purpose, compassion, and faith.

In the Bible my mother gave me, I recently came across a chapter in the book of Proverbs that spoke to me deeply about the importance of caring for our mothers. Proverbs chapter 23 provides wise counsel on honouring and respecting our mothers and why it is essential. This chapter underscores the significance of the mother-child relationship and the responsibilities that come with it. Proverbs 23 begins with an inspiring reminder to pay attention and listen to the teachings of our mothers. It urges us to treasure their words and store their instructions in our hearts.

This highlights the wisdom that mothers bring to our lives and the value of their guidance. As children, we must heed their advice and respect their authority, for they have our best interests at heart. The text emphasises that by following their teachings, we can lead a life of integrity and righteousness. The chapter warns against indulging in excess and becoming enticed by the world's pleasures. It cautions against gluttony, drunkenness, and chasing after riches, which can lead to ruin and destruction. Instead, it advocates moderation and self-control, urging us to focus on what truly matters. This reminds us that we should prioritise our relationships with our mothers above material possessions and earthly desires. Furthermore, Proverbs 23 emphasises the importance of showing our mothers' love and respect. Verse 22 states, "Listen to your father who gave your life, and do not despise your mother when she is old."

This verse underscores the lifelong bond between a mother and her child and the child's duty to honour and care for their mother, especially in her old age. It speaks to the value of intergenerational relationships and the need to cherish and support our mothers as they age. Another critical theme in Proverbs 23 is reaping what we sow. Verse 25 declares, "May your father and mother rejoice; may she who gave you birth be joyful!" This verse highlights the connection between honouring our parents and receiving blessings. By showing love and respect to our mothers, we bring them joy and happiness and invite blessings and favour into our lives.

This is a powerful reminder of the reciprocal nature of relationships and the importance of treating others with kindness and compassion. Proverbs chapter 23 offers valuable insights into the significance of caring for our mothers. It emphasises the need to listen to their wisdom, honour their teachings, and show them love and respect.

By following the guidance of this chapter, we can cultivate strong relationships with our mothers and experience the blessings that come from honouring them. As I reflect on these verses, I am reminded of my mother's profound impact on my life and the importance of cherishing and supporting her in return. May we all heed the wisdom of Proverbs 23 and honour our mothers as they deserve.

I Came Across the Book of Timothy

The importance of caring for our parents is a topic that is deeply ingrained in many cultures and religions around the world. In the book of 1 Timothy chapter 5, the apostle Paul addresses the issue of caring for widows in the church. However, his principles can be applied more broadly to honouring and caring for our parents. In this chapter, Paul instructs Timothy on addressing the needs of widows in the church community. He emphasises the importance of assisting widows in need and deserving of aid while encouraging those who can care for their family members.

This principle reflects that family members are responsible for caring for their parents in their old age and should not be shirked or neglected. Honouring and caring for our parents is rooted in respect, gratitude, and reciprocity. In many cultures, the bond between parents and their children is seen as sacred and fundamental to the fabric of society.

Parents are seen as the ones who brought us into this world, nurtured and raised us, and sacrificed their own needs and desires for the sake of their children. In return, it is only fitting and just that we honour and care for them in their old age when they can no longer care for themselves. This principle is reinforced in many religious and spiritual traditions as well. In Christianity, for example, the Bible teaches us that honouring one's parents is one of the Ten Commandments and that failing to do so is a severe transgression. Caring for our parents in their old age can take many forms, depending on their needs and circumstances. It may involve providing financial support, assisting with daily tasks, ensuring access to medical and emotional support, and simply spending quality time with them.

Regardless of the specifics, the underlying principle remains the same: we must honour and care for our parents to express gratitude for all they have done for us. In modern society, caring for our parents can be complicated by various factors such as distance, competing demands on our time and resources, and cultural attitudes towards ageing and dependency. In many Western societies, for example, there is a strong emphasis on individualism and self-reliance, making it difficult for people to prioritise caring for their parents over their own goals and ambitions. However, this should not be seen as an excuse to neglect our duty to our parents.

As our society grapples with issues such as an ageing population and increasing rates of loneliness and isolation among older people, the need to care for our parents becomes even more urgent. By honouring and caring for our parents, we not only fulfil a moral and spiritual obligation but also contribute to the well-being of our families and communities. The book of 1 Timothy chapter

5 provides essential guidance on the issue of caring for widows in the church. Still, its underlying principles can be applied more broadly to caring for our parents. The duty to honour and care for our parents is a fundamental aspect of many cultural, religious, and ethical traditions, and it is a responsibility that should be taken seriously and fulfilled to the best of our abilities. By doing so, we not only express our gratitude for all that our parents have done for us, but we also contribute to the well-being of our families and societies.

Footsteps of Grace

Generosity is a virtue that is often overlooked in today's fast-paced society. In a world where self-interest and individualism reign supreme, acts of kindness and selflessness are rare and precious. In times like these, we must pause and appreciate the people who have sacrificed their needs for our well-being. In my case, that person is my mother. My mother has always been my rock, confidante, and best friend. From a young age, she supported me through thick and thin, always putting my needs above hers. Whether staying up all night to help me with a school project or sacrificing her ambitions to ensure my success, my mother has always been there for me. She has shown me what true love and selflessness look like; I am eternally grateful for that.

As a token of my appreciation, I have decided to dedicate all sales generated from my book, "Footsteps of Grace," to my mother. This book, a collection of my reflections on life, love, and faith, is a labour of love that I am proud to share with the world. By donating all the proceeds to my mother, I want to show her how much she means to me and how grateful I am for all she has done.

My mother, being the humble and selfless person that she is, might not accept this gesture easily. She may argue that she does not need or deserve such a gift, that her love for me is unconditional and does not require repayment, but for me, this is not about repaying a debt or fulfilling an obligation. It is about tangibly expressing my gratitude and showing my mother how much her sacrifices have meant to me. I understand that no material gift can ever truly repay all that my mother has done for me. Her love, support, and guidance are priceless and irreplaceable. But by donating the proceeds from my book to her, I hope to honour her meaningfully and show her how much I appreciate everything she has done for me.

By dedicating "Footsteps of Grace" sales to my mother, I am expressing my gratitude and spreading love and kindness to others. By sharing my reflections and insights with the world, I aim to inspire others to appreciate the people who have made sacrifices for them and remind them that generosity, compassion, and selflessness are virtues worth cultivating in a cold and indifferent world.

As I embark on this journey of dedicating my book sales to my mother, I do so with a heart full of gratitude and a spirit of love. I am grateful for all that my mother has done for me, and I am honoured to be able to give back to her in this small way. Through this gesture, I want to show my mother how much she means to me and inspire others to express gratitude to the important people in their lives.

I vow that all sales generated from "Footsteps of Grace" will go directly to my mother as a token of my appreciation. I may never be able to repay her for all that she has done for me, but I can show her that her sacrifices have not gone unnoticed. My mother is my hero, inspiration, and guiding light, and I am grateful daily for her love and support. This gesture is the least I can do to express my gratitude and honour the amazing woman that she is.

A Letter to My Mother

Dear Nombulelo Monica Kumatana

I hope this letter finds you well. I am writing to express my deepest gratitude for the immeasurable love, guidance, and nurturing you have provided me. Your unwavering support and selfless dedication have profoundly shaped me, and I am eternally grateful for the sacrifices you made on my behalf. You have been a beacon of love and security since my earliest memories.

As my first teacher, you navigated me through life's complexities, teaching me invaluable compassion, integrity, and resilience lessons. Your love has been my stronghold, encouraging me to face challenges head-on, surmount obstacles, and pursue my dreams fervently. In every moment of uncertainty, you have been my steadfast rock, offering comfort and a listening ear when I needed it most. Your unwavering faith in me has bolstered my confidence, enabling me to realise my potential and embrace my true self. Within your nurturing embrace, I have found peace and understanding. Your gentle guidance has underscored the importance of kindness, empathy, and the transformative power of a caring gesture. Your patience and acceptance played a crucial role in shaping me into someone who cherishes love, respect, and inclusivity. No words can fully convey my appreciation or encapsulate my boundless love and admiration for you. For all your efforts, visible and unseen, I offer my heartfelt thanks. I am forever thankful for your endless sacrifices, the nights you spent awake for my sake, and the unconditional love you bestowed upon me. Your presence has been the greatest gift, reminding me of the special bond between a mother and her child.

Today, I honour you not just as my mother but as an exemplary figure, a confidante, and the pillar of my strength. You are an extraordinary woman; I am proud to be your child.

Your Loving Son.

Psalm 16:11

You will show me the path of life; in Your presence is fullness of joy; at Your right hand are pleasures forevermore.

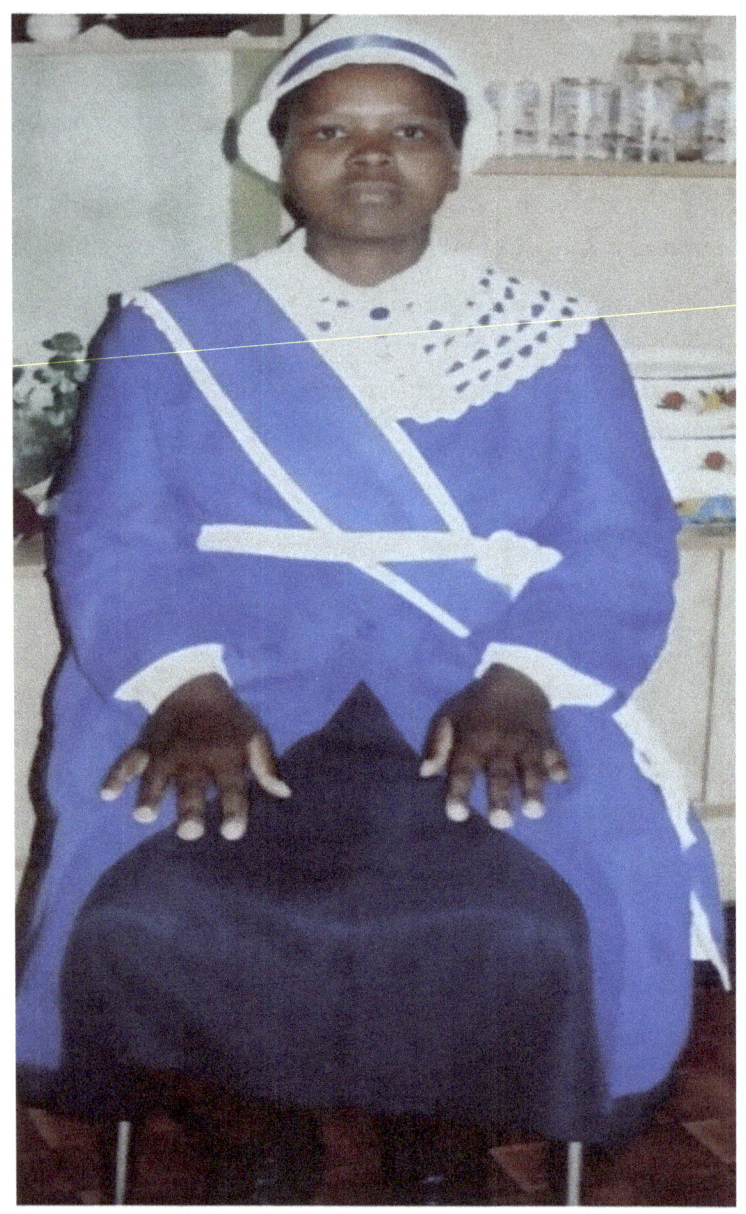

www.ingramcontent.com/pod-product-compliance
Lightning Source LLC
Chambersburg PA
CBHW072012290426
44109CB00018B/2217